*Faith, Hope, and Love
in the Technological Society*

FAITH, HOPE, *and* LOVE
in the Technological Society

Franz A. Foltz
Frederick A. Foltz

CASCADE *Books* • Eugene, Oregon

FAITH, HOPE, AND LOVE IN THE TECHNOLOGICAL SOCIETY

Copyright © 2018 Franz A. Foltz and Frederick A. Foltz. All rights reserved. Except for brief quotations in critical publications or reviews, no part of this book may be reproduced in any manner without prior written permission from the publisher. Write: Permissions, Wipf and Stock Publishers, 199 W. 8th Ave., Suite 3, Eugene, OR 97401.

Cascade Books
An Imprint of Wipf and Stock Publishers
199 W. 8th Ave., Suite 3
Eugene, OR 97401

www.wipfandstock.com

PAPERBACK ISBN: 978-1-5326-3625-7
HARDCOVER ISBN: 978-1-5326-3627-1
EBOOK ISBN: 978-1-5326-3626-4

Cataloguing-in-Publication data:

Names: Foltz, Franz A., author. | Foltz, Frederick A., author.

Title: Faith, hope, and love in the technological society. / Franz A. Foltz and Frederick A. Foltz.

Description: Eugene, OR: Cascade Books, 2018 | Includes bibliographical references and index.

Identifiers: ISBN 978-1-5326-3625-7 (paperback) | ISBN 978-1-5326-3627-1 (hardcover) | ISBN 978-1-5326-3626-4 (ebook)

Subjects: LCSH: Religion and science. | Technology—Religious aspects—Christianity.

Classification: BL240.3 .F68 2018 (print) | BL240 (ebook)

Manufactured in the U.S.A.   JULY 26, 2018

Scripture quotations are from the New Revised Standard Version Bible, copyright 1989 by the Division of Christian Education of the National Council of Churches of Christ in the USA and used by permission.

To Sheila and Faith Ann, Gabriel and Jacob, Freda and Frances, who share and enrich our lives.

Table of Contents

Preface ix

Acknowledgements xi

Introduction xiii

1. The Technological Society 1
2. Christianity in the Technological Society 21
3. Words and Meaning 46
4. Interaction 65
5. Faith 80
6. Hope 102
7. Love 124
8. Connections 146
9. So What? 162

Bibliography 169

Index 177

Preface

IN HIS 1985 WORK, *Humiliation of the Word,* Jacques Ellul claimed, "Anyone wishing to save humanity today must first of all save the word."[1] He was lamenting that by replacing words with images, modern technology was destroying the "blessed uncertainty of language," and with it, qualities regarded as essential to human culture.[2]

Bringing together concerns from Ellul's sociological and theological work, the statement itself contains the ambiguity Ellul thought necessary for creative thinking and decision-making. *Salvation*, a term usually associated with religion, is applied to social work. *Word*, in this context, could refer to simple human discourse or divine communication. "Saving humanity" can be read as insuring the survival of the human race, preserving features that make life worth living, or, for that matter, the ultimate redeeming of the creation. What seems on the surface to be an observation about social relationships is loaded with religious significance.

In many ways, our book simply ponders the meaning of Ellul's profound statement. For many years we've discussed how modern technology affects Christian thought and practice, Franz as a scholar, studying science, technology, and society, and Fritz as a pastor, teaching Lutheran theology. After publishing a number of articles on the topic, we decided it was time to bring some of our insights together in book form. We decided to do this by examining how modern technology has affected the use of faith, hope, and love, the three words Christianity has used to describe its lifestyle for over 2,000 years.

Ellul's statement quite naturally caught our attention. After twenty-five years, his warning is more prescient than ever. We have seen how the

---

1. Ellul, *Humiliation of the Word*, 254.
2. Ellul, *Humiliation of the Word*, 18.

Preface

Internet, the cell phone, and Facebook have further changed the way we use words. They enable us to exchange information easily, but often obscure rather than clarify meaning. Words are now replaced with emojis, as well as scientific images and formulae. Narratives indicate how the writer feels without any presumption of searching for a common truth.

This humiliation of the word significantly impacts religion, which depends on the richness of words to make sense of our relationship with God. All three of the major Western religions proclaim that God not only creates though speech, but also continues to relate to his people with words. Ernst Cassirer claimed that "almost all great cultural religions" picture the word as either the tool that the creator god employs, or the primary source from which he creates. Cassirer cites a passage from the Taittiriya Brahm as a superb example: "On the spoken word all the gods depend, all beasts and men, in the word live all creation . . . . The word is the navel of the divine world."[3]

Judaism and Christianity have also perceived technology's challenge to language. The Babel story in Genesis 11:1–9 describes one feature of the good order God established in the creation as "the whole earth had one language and the same words." The implication is clearly that people, like God, had the power to speak and create good things. However, they used their potential to "make a name for themselves" by building a tower to reach into the heavens. This failure to use God's gift appropriately is pictured as a return to the chaos previous to God's creation. Confusion reigns when the inhabitants can no longer speak the same language. Words separate rather than bring the people together.

---

3. Cassirer, *Language and Myth*, 45–48.

Acknowledgements

WE OWE MUCH TO the members of our family—both biological and spiritual—with whom we have eaten and conversed. We have shared many nourishing meals with many wonderful people in our homes, at conferences, and in other special gatherings.

We owe special thanks to the late Rustum Roy, who started us on this path almost thirty-five years ago. His leadership within the greater Science, Technology, and Society (STS) community through the creation of the Technological Literacy Conference and the *Bulletin* for STS allowed us to connect with many of the others who helped in this journey. He was especially instrumental by bringing the Illich group to State College in the late 1980s. The younger of us shared many meals with Ivan Illich, Barbara Duden, Jean Robert, Wolfgang Sachs, and the many others who gathered together to discuss our technological society.

For that matter, we need to acknowledge how important the entire Science, Technology, and Society community has been to our journey. Our particular part of that interdisciplinary group regards its work as a mission to preserve human values in an environment dominated by science and technology. Although we are frequently characterized as Luddites, we in no way disparage the great contributions of modern technology. We simply believe it is essential to recognize its limitations, and even dark sides. Much of our work grew from conversations over dinner with that community, especially with Willem Vanderburg, Richard Stivers, James van der Laan, and all the others with whom we gathered over the last two decades in Baltimore, Toronto, and Rochester.

Richard Stivers deserves special mention as he continually encouraged us to write the book and offered welcomed recommendations when carefully reviewing it. We both cherish his friendship.

ACKNOWLEDGEMENTS

We also owe special thanks to our granddaughter and niece, Kayla Martine, who turned our thoughts into a readable form. We first sought her help as a time-saving measure, but soon found she was invaluable in composing a creative work. Family is extremely important to us, and she provided delight in making this an even larger family project.

Introduction

OUR WORK WILL FOCUS on faith, hope, and love, often described as the attributes needed for living the Christian life. These three words provide a common narrative, enabling believers to understand and express their religious experiences. Connecting the past and future with the present, they provide a historical context for making decisions.

Traditionally, theologians have labeled the triad the theological virtues, in contrast to the moral or cardinal virtues of justice, courage, prudence, and temperance. Unlike the moral virtues that are derived from nature and discerned by human reason, the theological virtues are defined as gifts of the Holy Spirit that transform human faculties so they can participate in the divine life.

Paul describes them as pure gift. If moral virtues are available through natural reason common to all people, the theological virtues depend on action initiated by God. The apostle claimed that Christ pours them into believers' hearts while they are still weak, sinners, and even enemies of God. Throughout our study, we shall speak of God speaking the opening words of the divine-human conversation.

> Therefore, since we are justified by faith, we have peace with God through our Lord Jesus Christ, through whom we have obtained access to this grace in which we stand; and we boast in our hope of sharing the glory of God . . . . [H]ope does not disappoint us, because God's love has been poured into our hearts through the Holy Spirit that has been given to us . . . . God proves his love for us in that while we still were sinners Christ died for us . . . . For if while we were enemies, we were reconciled to God through the death of his Son, much more surely, having been reconciled, will we be saved by his life.[1]

1. Rom 5:11.

Introduction

This is the basis of Thomas Aquinas's definition of the theological virtues as infused grace that supplement, rather than supplant, the moral virtues. Pope Emeritus Benedict XVI follows suit when he claims these virtues direct human reason in the right direction.[2]

Virtues are general traits or qualities that maintain the "blessed ambiguity" of language that Ellul lauds. Their beauty is comprehensiveness, not specificity. For instance, courage can mean stand and fight, try another risky tactic, turn the other cheek, or, sometimes, flee. All depends on the particular situation. This flexibility provides relevance in the midst of changing circumstance. It resists any kind of reductionism that would diminish the fullness of reality or the uniqueness of any of its parts.

Like the other virtues, faith, hope, and love operate a lot like habits of the heart. Without much thought, we constantly employ them to describe who we are, to whom we belong, for what we hope, and how we should act, but we also have difficulty analyzing how they operate. Trying to explain precisely what is taken for granted often obscures rather than clarifies.

Much of our book will examine how our technological society hears each of the three words by themselves and in combination. However, before doing that, we need to make clear how we define technology and Christianity. Franz will examine technology relying heavily on his teachers Jacques Ellul, Rustum Roy, and Ivan Illich. Fritz will attempt to represent the voice of traditional Christianity, perhaps a futile task, using biblical theology based on Luther's theology of the cross. Both perspectives are by nature contrarian, a helpful position for critiquing our secular technological society. In conclusion, we shall attempt to offer some suggestions for recovering the role of the three theological virtues in providing meaning for the church and our society.

---

2. Benedict XVI, "Spe Salvi," #7, #23–26.

1

The Technological Society

Until recently, technology was defined as the tools humans used to enhance their labor. It was assumed that each new tool overcame another natural limitation. Society marked its progress by advancements in technology, characterizing each stage of civilization by its tools. At a young age, students were taught about the Stone, Bronze, and Iron Ages. Older students divided modernity into the Age of the Printing Press, the Machine, the Automobile, and the Computer. It was expected that the next technical innovation would solve many, if not all, of humanity's present problems.

People understood that each new tool brought some changes to the world in which we live, forcing society to conform to its nature and causing modifications in lifestyles. As the saying goes, if all I have is a hammer, everything looks like a nail. It was assumed that the change would be an improvement. A simple tool would increase bodily strength. A complicated machine would surmount obstacles of time and space.

Today we have entered a new technological age, characterized by electronic machines and systems. It is no longer a matter of picking up a primitive tool to perform a specific task. This new technology shapes our world and pervades our lives far more decisively. As soon as we wake, we begin pushing buttons to turn on lights, heat food, and fire up computers. Throughout the day, we are constantly connected to systems, such as the electric grid and the Internet. Before we go to bed we turn off some of our connections, but many systems continue to serve us. Even as we sleep, thermostats regulate heating, lights provide security, and computers receive messages.

This has led some to question if every new technology really enriches human life. They are increasingly aware that while modern devices might increase the quality of some aspects, they also diminish others. The telegraph, for instance, enabled people to communicate with tremendous speed over great distances, but in doing so it removed body language and facial expressions from the conversation.

Others wonder whether we control modern technologies or they control us. We adjust to their requirements when we electrify our houses, drive our cars, and use the Internet. No matter how prudent we desire to be, we find ourselves constantly buying the latest devices. Ten years is ancient in the electronic age, and the system will not service "outdated" devices. Perhaps we are no longer masters of our technologies.

Three Speeches

A brief look at three commencement speeches indicates how much our society's perception of technology has shifted over the past century. By examining these excerpts, we shall see how this perception has morphed basic concepts and words that traditionally defined our society. Each speaker presented a view of technology consistent with his time period.

JFK and the Technocratic 1960s

When the older of the authors received a graduate degree from Yale in 1962, the President of the United States, John Fitzgerald Kennedy, delivered the commencement address. He used the occasion to champion technology as the means to a better, happier, more rational society. All of our problems had become "technical and administrative."[1] He observed that this meant, "In our own time we must move on from the reassuring repetition of stale phrases to a new, difficult, but essential confrontation with reality."

Kennedy identified these stale phrases as the truisms, stereotypes, and clichés of philosophies and ideologies. Although he never mentioned religion, it certainly fits his understanding of old-fashioned ideas that lead to clashes rather than unity. In place of these, he maintained that the "ways and means of reaching common goals" had become the "practical management of a modern economy."

1. Kennedy, "Commencement Address."

The president ended by acknowledging that depending on technical rather than ideological reasoning necessitated the confidence that all major elements of our society would live up to their responsibilities. His last paragraph spoke of what would enable this to happen:

> But the unfortunate fact of the matter is that our rhetoric has not kept pace with the speed of social and economic change. Discussion is essential. Nearly 150 years ago Thomas Jefferson wrote, "The new circumstances under which we are placed call for new words, new phrases, and for the transfer of old words to new objects." New words, new phrases, the transfer of old words to new objects—that is truer today than it was in the time of Jefferson, because the role of this country is now vastly more significant. There is a show in England called "Stop the World, I Want to Get Off." You have not chosen to exercise that option. You are part of the world, and you must participate in these days of our years in the solution of the problems that pour upon us, requiring the most sophisticated and technical judgment; and as we work in consonance to meet the authentic problems of our times, we will generate a vision and an energy which will demonstrate anew to the world the superior vitality and strength of the free society.[2]

The 1962 audience and press regarded JFK's address as cutting edge. Many historians still regard it as a major speech. It certainly reflected the times. The United States was focused on putting a man on the moon. Only a few years later, the nation turned to technology as a means of accomplishing President Johnson's Great Society. Not long after that, Bill Clinton expressed the same confidence in technology when he welcomed the new age of nanotechnology as bringing the solution to all of humanity's problems.[3]

Kennedy's address assumed that the solution of modern problems was beyond the ability of ordinary people. He promised to gather specialists who were up to the task. One of those experts, former Secretary of Defense Robert McNamara, has come to epitomize the position that every problem can be solved by technocratic means. He defined the Pentagon as a group of technicians solving military problems rather than a group of politicians. As that approach has taken over all areas of government, it has effectively taken public decision-making in all matters out of the hands of ordinary citizens. Supposedly, only experts who specialize in a discipline have the

---

2. Kennedy, "Commencement Address."
3. Clinton, "Nanotechnology Initiative."

knowledge and skills necessary to make decisions and regulate practices in that area.

JFK's commencement address also assumed that the rise of technology has to be accompanied by the denigration of tradition. Belief systems, described as philosophy and ideology, should not play a role in modern decision-making because they cause conflict and stand in the way of progress. To the contrary, the bulk of our work will argue that belief systems are essential for the vision and energy necessary for direction and purpose in making life's important decisions. To destroy belief systems is to lose the very resources needed for a meaningful democratic society. A society must be very careful when creating new words or phrases, and especially when transferring old words to new objects. Too often we end up "worshipping" an automobile.

A LEGO World in the 1990s

When the younger author received his doctorate from Rensselaer Polytechnic Institute in 1996, the commencement speaker was Peter Eio, President of LEGO/Dacta Systems, the largest toy manufacturer in the world. The significance of this speech was not the particular words spoken, but the speaker himself. There is nothing wrong with manufacturing toys. However, until recently, it would be very strange for a university to illustrate its fundamental values with the CEO of a company that makes toys. The value, of course, was not toy making but rather the efficient use of blocks as an educational tool. The award recognized that *technique* had become a value unto itself, especially for its role in stimulating the economy.

In the 1990 world, technology was controlled by a corporate-government elite who projected their worldview onto all aspects of living, even play. It was the dawn of the dot-com age, a time when researchers could get rich simply on the promise of biotechnology before producing anything at all. Technology was no longer the means to a better world. It was the end in and of itself.

The 1996 audience thought that the toy maker was cutting edge. The assumptions of the Kennedy speech are in part what led to this. When technology is hailed as the answer to all our problems and tradition is regarded as old-fashioned and useless, society ends up with industry and economics determining all, even academic and religious values. In a technocracy, learning becomes fundable research, purpose is defined by economic goals, and worth is measured by providing new products that provide jobs and keep the economy growing.

President Obama and 2010

A further change in society's thinking is reflected in the commencement speech made about fifteen years later by the President of the United States at Hampton University. Barack Obama, like the former two commencement speakers, spoke of this being

> a period of breathtaking change, like few others in our history. We can't stop these changes, but we can channel them, we can shape them, we can adapt to them. And education is what can allow us to do so. It can fortify you, as it did earlier generations, to meet the tests of your own time.[4]

However, he spoke of education as far more than technical training.

> Your education has honed your research abilities, sharpened your analytical powers, given you a context for understanding the world. Those skills will come in handy. But the goal was always to teach you something more. Over the past four years, you've argued both sides of a debate. You've read novels and histories that take different cuts at life.[5]

Someone, hopefully a faculty member, shouted "Amen" at this point.

Obama then described this essential education as "opening your mind; of helping you understand what it's like to walk in somebody else's shoes," values that we associate with traditional liberal arts. He described these as essential for passing "the elemental test of any democracy: whether people with differing points of view can learn from each other, and work with each other, and find a way forward together." To make sure that he was understood, he referred to the limitations of technology.

> And meanwhile, you're coming of age in a 24/7 media environment that bombards us with all kinds of content and exposes us to all kinds of arguments, some of which don't always rank that high on the truth meter. And with iPods and iPads; and XBoxes and PlayStations—none of which I know how to work—[laughter]—information becomes a distraction, a diversion, a form of

---

4. Obama, "Commencement Speech."
5. Obama, "Commencement Speech."

entertainment, rather than a tool of empowerment, rather than the means of emancipation. So all of this is not only putting pressure on you; it's putting new pressure on our country and on our democracy.... With so many voices clamoring for attention on blogs, and on cable, on talk radio, it can be difficult, at times, to sift through it all; to know what to believe; to figure out who's telling the truth and who's not. Let's face it; even some of the craziest claims can quickly gain traction. I've had some experience in that regard.[6]

Like Kennedy, Obama used Thomas Jefferson to support his argument, but in an entirely different manner. He cited the third president's words used in support of education, "If a nation expects to be ignorant and free, it expects what never was and never will be." Obama went on:

> What Jefferson recognized, like the rest of that gifted founding generation, was that in the long run their improbable experiment—called America—wouldn't work if its citizens were uninformed.... It could only work if each of us stayed informed and engaged; if we held our government accountable; if we fulfilled the obligations of citizenship. They understood that the success of their experiment depended on the participation of its people—the participation of Americans like all of you. The participation of all those who have ever sought to perfect our union.[7]

Obama used Jefferson's words to argue that a liberal arts education that imparts wisdom is just as important as one in science and technology that provides knowledge. Proper participation in democratic decision-making involves not only having sufficient information, but even more the judgment to evaluate and use that data appropriately.

Changing Technological Views

These three speeches reflect the way that thought has changed in the last fifty years. Kennedy's words reflected his society, which placed faith in technology's ability to solve all our problems. His words echoed the slogan of the 1933–1934 Chicago World's Fair: "Science finds, Industry applies, and Man conforms." They can be heard as determinism put into entrepreneurial terms: "If we don't do it, someone else will." All depends on following the findings of science and the needs of industry. There is no place for purpose

6. Obama, "Commencement Speech."
7. Obama, "Commencement Speech."

and no time for precautionary principles. We cannot afford to wait. We must rely on technology's promise to fix its mistakes.

Offering an honorary degree to Eio illustrated how much this technological development had become attached to economic values. Even technology designed for children supported the economic-technological worldview. Kennedy made it clear that managing economic growth was vital to the common good. Eio was honored for expanding this view to all aspects of society, even educational play. Technology was everything.

Obama called for a different approach, one that used wisdom and judgment to develop and use technology for the common good. He championed the liberal arts, claiming that they provided the compassion and critical thought necessary for making sense of the proliferation of information in today's society. Noting that the constant bombardment of electronic media often obscures the truth, he reminded his audience that the arts had always supplied the wisdom necessary to use information and power for the common good. They had established the canons necessary to prioritize and evaluate according to the values of the culture. In contrast to Kennedy, who dismissed these standards as old-fashioned, Obama appealed to the humanities for guidance in setting priorities for using technology to tackle the basic problems of humankind.

Obama's speech was as much a reflection of the time as the other two. Kennedy's was the age of the space race and nuclear energy. Eio's age was the biotech revolution as well as the birth of the Internet. Obama's age came after the bursting of the dot-com bubble and the world financial collapse of 2008.

Nonetheless, Obama's speech was much more controversial than the other two. The national press accused him of bad-mouthing technology at a time when we needed it more than ever. Pretty much all of the coverage chided the president for being a Luddite. One after another, reporters and commentators spoke of how often each day they used their BlackBerrys to get information. Few seemed to understand that Obama was speaking of far more weighty concerns when he called for education that provides the wisdom to use information appropriately in confronting the basic human problems that surround us.

Technology in Society

The debate reflected in these speeches highlights some profound questions about the nature of modern technology that a small number of scholars began to address long before President Kennedy spoke at Yale. Most of the time their critiques have been dismissed with the same type of arguments that pundits used against President Obama.

Critiques of Technology

The best known of these scholars is Jacques Ellul, whose classic treatment of these questions in *The Technological Society* laid the groundwork for all subsequent studies. His main thesis contended that modern technology has become so powerful and all-pervasive that it has formed an environment to accommodate its needs. That which was designed to help us overcome our limitations has imposed its own controls on us. We are forced to conform.

At first that argument flies in the face of all that we have been taught about modern technology. Popular opinion celebrates with President Kennedy the freedom it supposedly has made possible. Each new innovation is presumed to offer new possibilities from which we can choose. Ellul argued that a closer look reveals that all these options must fit the technological environment. A simplistic example is the great variety of products offered in a supermarket. Standing before the many, many different kinds of cereal seems to present many choices, at first. However, after a little thought, it becomes apparent that almost all of the options are pretty much the same. Further investigation finds that many are the very same product made by the same company, just sold under different brand names.

A more far-reaching example is the interstate highway system. The decision to make the car our primary form of transportation led to the formation of an environment that eventually demanded a restructuring of our lives. Highways, strip malls, the proliferation of gas stations and garages, the creation of fast-food restaurants, and the expansion of the suburbs became necessary. Once that infrastructure (which costs great amounts of money and time to maintain) became entrenched, it became nearly impossible to live without a car. You needed it to get to work, buy groceries, visit friends, attend school, and all the other activities associated with a "normal" life.

Accepting the car meant not only accepting the system that accommodated it, but also rejecting all other options. The demand it created for continual inputs of tremendous sums of money precluded public financing for other forms of transportation, such as mass transit. And once the infrastructure was in place, other developments naturally followed. People found it convenient to move to the suburbs, shop at malls, and eat at McDonald's. Once you make the car the primary form of transportation, you are forced to accept the rest.

It does not take much effort to see the same monopolistic characteristics in the adoption of any modern technology, whether electricity, digital storage, computer systemization, nuclear energy, or pharmaceutical medicine. Each creates an environment that forces all to adjust to its needs.

A second scholar regarded as a pioneer in the study of technology is the social critic Ivan Illich. He is best known for showing how modern society has transformed natural human activities into institutions, which he depicted as systems having a life of their own. Illich was renowned for demonstrating how these systems become counterproductive when they inevitably end up working against the original intentions of those who created them.

Illich, a specialist in twelfth-century civilization, was speaking of crossing a historical line where our use of technology changed qualitatively as well as quantitatively. Before we crossed this line, our decisions were made on the basis of how they would affect other people and the environment. After crossing it, we are forced also to consider the effects of technology on every decision we make. It is no longer simply a matter of what people do with tools, but also what tools do to people.

You can readily perceive how this happens by pondering what takes place in the development of weapons from clubs to atomic bombs, energy from campfires to electricity, and modes of communication from pencils to computers. There is a world of difference between placing a knife or a gun in someone's hand. Because the gun overcomes the limitations of distance, time, and power, killing becomes tremendously easier. This difference is exacerbated further with more powerful weaponry. Before crossing Illich's threshold, it was taken for granted that "people not guns kill people." This is much harder to argue now, as most people understand the qualitative difference between using a single-shot .22 rifle and an AK-47 assault weapon, or, for that matter, a terrorist bomb. Illich described this difference as an institutionalization of values, in which the speed, size, and power of technology place most decision-making entirely in the hands of large establishments.

Technique and Society

Both Ellul and Illich are continually described as being opposed to technological change. Their numerous critics accuse them of denying the great benefits modern tools, techniques, and technologies have provided for society. Technology has enabled us to eliminate wastes in time, energy, and money while meeting many desired goals. Inevitably, the critics cite how much everyone in the developed world has gained from medicine's ability to extend and enrich life. The tools in the operating room enable a surgeon to do magnificent work. The standardized techniques involved can be quickly and easily spread to other operating rooms throughout the world. These tools and techniques enable an average physician to perform procedures once confined to the most skilled specialist.

The criticism notes that none of this would be possible without the extreme power provided by technological systems. A laptop computer is a tool that standing alone has limited usefulness. Loaded with software and connected to millions of servers and other computers via a Wi-Fi connection, it becomes a tremendously powerful system. Because this vast system includes millions of miles of fiber optics and various other cables, millions of other users with their computers, routers, servers, and lots of other things about which we have no idea, it is an incredibly potent technology. The portable laptop computer allows the common person to store, sort, retrieve, and utilize vast amounts of information.

Ellul and Illich readily agree. They are not denigrating technology, but describing the social phenomenon that has taken place in the modern age as thought forms previously limited to specialized functions in problem-solving have been extended into every factor of people's lives. Ellul refers to this as *technique*.

> The term *technique,* as I used the term, does not mean machines, technology, or this or that procedure for attaining an end. In our technological society, technique is the *totality of methods rationally arrived at and having absolute efficiency* (for a given stage of development) in *every field of human activity.* Its characteristics are new; the technique of the present has no common measure with that of the past.[8]

He listed two essential characteristics: 1) "In whatever the aspect of the domain in which it is applied, a rational process is present which tends

---

8. Ellul, *The Technological Society,* xxv, 19.

to bring mechanics to bear on all that is spontaneous or irrational . . . . There is the reduction of method to its logical dimension alone. Every intervention of *technique* is, in effect, a reduction of facts, forces, phenomena, means, and instruments to the schema of logic" and 2) "The world that is being created by the accumulation of technical means is an artificial world and hence radically different from the natural world."[9]

In 1993, Illich acknowledged that Ellul's understanding of *la technique* had played a central part in his work ever since he read *The Technological Society* in 1965.

> I have adopted this Ellulian concept because it permits me to identify—in education, transport, modern medical and scientific activities—the threshold at which these projects absorb, conceptually and physically, the client into the tool; the threshold where the products of consumption change into things which themselves consume; the threshold where the milieu of technique transforms into numbers those who are entrapped in it; the threshold where technology is decisively transformed into Moloch, the system.[10]

It is important to clarify that *technique* is different from a technique or a set of techniques. Throughout the rest of our work we shall take care to speak of tools as things we can touch, like a hammer or a laptop, techniques as standardized, scientifically based methods for solving problems, a technology as a system or set of systems that integrate tools and techniques, and italicized *technique* as a concept describing how all of these have affected the way we live in the present age.

Our study of technology's effect on the Christian virtues assumes that *technique* is a sociological phenomenon much as Ellul and Illich defined it. However, it will soon become evident that we also speak of it as the ideology of the technological society. In *The Technological Bluff*, Ellul referred to scientism as the ideology that supports *technique*.[11] In *Technology and Magic: The Triumph of the Irrational*, Richard Stivers described technological utopianism as the myth of a technological civilization that provides a sense of the sacred promising survival and health.[12] For our purposes, when you refer to a totality of methods in which efficiency trumps every other value, you are speaking of an ideology, at least an ideology understood as a creed

---

9. Ellul, *The Technological Society*, 78–79.
10. Illich, "To Honor Jacques Ellul," 3.
11. Ellul, *The Technological Bluff*, 172–88.
12. Stivers, *Technology and Magic*, 125–36.

assumed in a particular historical period. We think this understanding of *technique* is quite evident in the Kennedy speech.

Connections and Context

Examining in depth Ellul's two characteristics of *technique* offers a foundation from which to study technology's effect on the Christian virtues. The first, as noted above, claims "Every intervention of technique is, in effect, a reduction of facts, forces, phenomena, means, and instruments to the schema of logic." Ellul described this as a rational process "which tends to bring mechanics to bear on all that is spontaneous or irrational . . . ."[13]

William Vandenberg and Richard Stivers have written extensively about technology removing people and things from their natural contexts. A technique breaks everything into parts, isolating them from each other and eliminating anything that does not directly serve as an efficient means for solving the problem at hand. That means focusing only on the specific task and not the context in which it appears. A technique by definition only considers the parts of a problem that suit its project and disregards everything else. That works well in an artificial system or machine, where parts can be manipulated and rearranged like Lego blocks, but not in real-life situations involving human beings.

A world characterized by *technique* reduces all to technical means that seem to be the most efficient operations in the artificial world that it has created. Consequently, it ignores a great deal of reality and life by breaking natural connections to nature, place, time, and community.

Perhaps in reaction to this development, "connection" has recently become a buzzword that expresses people's desire for unity. Cognitive scientists speak of the brain's "connectedness." Sociologists regard "connectiveness" as a desirable characteristic of social networking. At first, technology would seem to facilitate these connections by overcoming the limitations of time and space. However, on closer examination it becomes evident that *technique* always breaks connections to everything not directly related to the problem at hand. At this point, we shall very quickly introduce various ways *technique* breaks natural connections, promising to develop these more fully in the remainder of our work.

---

13. Ellul, *The Technological Society*, 78–79.

Breaking the Connection to Nature

Throughout most of our history, human life was immersed in nature. The natural world was a given to which people adjusted. They planned their days around its weather. They sailed their ships in its winds and currents. They learned lessons from its processes. Shakespeare could write that people found "tongues in trees, books in the running brooks, sermons in stones, and good in everything."[14] Philosophers could speak of a natural reason. People attempted to live in harmony with the natural environment.

Today, technology attempts to overcome the limitations that nature imposes on us. After a long career exploring the relationship between science and religion, Philip Hefner maintained that the present biotech worldview is founded on the premise that all nature should be reshaped in ways that human beings deem desirable.[15]

As a consequence of this effort, most of us spend more time in a technological environment than in a natural one. This is so widespread that many urbanites are frightened of the darkness and movements of wildlife in rural areas, sights and sounds that were once regarded as the beauty of the earth. This makes it easier for many to regard nature as simply a resource to be mined in fueling the needs of our technology.

Bill McKibben addressed this issue in his book *The End of Nature* when he claimed that it is difficult to know what is natural anymore. Traditional ethics used natural birth and natural death as criteria for judging the beginning and ending of life situations. Natural birth meant enduring the pain of childbirth without the benefit of drugs. Natural death meant allowing things such as dire illness and injury to take their course without interruption. These criteria are not much help in our technological society, in which modern medicine uses all sorts of procedures to overcome a couple's infertility or to ensure the life of a very premature baby. Using extreme surgical and chemical means to prolong life is hardly letting things take their natural course.

Breaking Connection to Place

Until fairly recently people were identified by name and place, for example Jesus of Nazareth. Even today we introduce ourselves by mentioning our

---

14. Shakespeare, *As You Like It*, II.i.563–64.
15. Hefner, *The Human Factor*.

neighborhood, town, state, region, and nation. This was natural, as most people were born, lived, and died in the same location. They lived off the land and found what they needed nearby.

Presently, technology enables and often forces people to move from place to place. It allows them to communicate immediately with others thousands of miles away. In fact, sometimes people have more contact with friends living in distant places than they have with their next-door neighbors. Beyond that, we are increasingly dependent on faraway places for just about everything we use: our food, our clothing, and our slews of manufactured possessions.

At a recent International Society of Science, Technology, and Society conference, a Korean participant described how his nation was reeling because it had lost its identity as a people. In a very short time span, its story had changed from a Korean, to an American, to a technology narrative. He characterized the latter as devastating because it made efficiency and practical necessity the standard for everything while denigrating the traditions, customs, and values by which his people knew themselves and on which their community was based.

Breaking the Connection to Time

In the past, people were shaped by the customs and traditions in their culture. A great deal of their education involved studying these ways of life. History was regarded as a meaningful narrative that people were encouraged to remember in order to know who they were, what they were to believe, and what they were to do.

Technique offers a "culture of now" that pretty much disregards the past. That often is a good thing, as it corrects the parochialism, prejudice, and oppressive structures that often characterized past societies. However, it also discounts the wisdom of the past that provided meaning and purpose. Politics, defined as making decisions that enable humans to accomplish what they want, have just about replaced philosophies and belief systems that once provided social and moral standards for making those decisions.

The only value of the past is the information that it contributes for solving the immediate problem at hand. The promise of the future is primarily the new opportunities that it offers to pursue more personal happiness. Those who have benefited most from technology generally work hard to preserve the status quo. In the context of our present global society, this has come to mean maintaining what the First World enjoys and working to provide more of it. Poor countries are described as developing nations whose goal is to become like those in the First World.

Breaking the Connection with Community

Perhaps the most critical break for Christianity is the loss of our connection with community. All sorts of studies have traced the loss of community in the past fifty years. They usually attempt to explain how we have moved from persons who know themselves by their relationships with their neighbors to a group of isolated individuals. Almost always technology is mentioned as a primary factor, even if it is not examined closely.

Critics of such studies usually champion electronic social networking as a modern improvement. However, it takes little effort to observe that these relationships are narrow, bland, and impersonal. They thrive on individuals simply reporting to one another what they are presently doing, thinking, and feeling. This is hardly a mode of conversation that involves the commitment and vulnerability of traditional community. To proclaim "I love you" over electronic media does not come close to saying it face-to-face while holding hands. Although most people speak continually of this loss, few can extract themselves from the situation. Their cell phone vibrates, indicating a text message, and they immediately break off a conversation to answer it.

An Artificial World

Both Ellul and Illich maintain that this reductionism inherent in *technique* has created an artificial world that is "radically different from the natural world."[16] As can readily be perceived in their impassioned word choice, both scholars believe this new period of history presents dangerous challenges largely undiscerned. Although Ellul looks at it as an artificial environment or world and Illich analyzes it in terms of self-destructive institutional systems, both believe that we live in an entirely new epoch in which traditional ethical standards, spiritual considerations, and cultural values no longer play a relevant role in the decision-making of either institutions or persons.

16. Ellul, *The Technological Society*, 78–79.

When citing his agreement with Ellul's characterization of this era as a "completely unique historical extravagance," Illich wrote:

> This is clearly seen when we wish to raise ethical questions. Manifestly, the moral term "evil" is not applicable to documented events such as the Shoah, Hiroshima, or the current attempts at artificial reproduction of human-like creatures. These repugnant, abominable, horrifying enterprises cannot be debated. One cannot make them grammatical subjects. Every enquiry about such things, whether they are feasible or not, just or unjust, good or evil, legitimizes the status of inexpressible horror. Those are extreme examples. Reading Ellul makes one understand that the immersion of daily life in a *milieu technique* places one no less beyond good and evil.[17]

This is an astonishing charge. At the least it asserts that meaning and purpose have no place in *technique*'s thought world because, as we heard in JFK's address, they lead to conflict rather than cooperation. At the most, it means that technical force is all that remains, and that the only thing left to oppose it is another technical force.[18] The NRA slogan "The only thing that can stop a bad man with a gun is a good man with a gun" makes perfect sense, because there is nothing more to consider.

Modern weapons systems illustrate Illich's point. Although governmental leaders still cite just war theory to justify their actions, these classic rules of war are no longer relevant in the environment of ICBM-launched atomic bombs. Precepts about hope for success and restoring peace are meaningless when nations are forced to spend vast amounts of money to maintain a constant state of war. Stipulations about proportionality of force and avoiding harm to civilians are senseless when nonmilitary causalities have become necessary collateral damage. Consider that 90 percent of the causalities in modern warfare are civilians and only one civilian was killed out of the 50,000 slain in the Battle of Gettysburg. This civilian death was regarded as so extraordinary that Jenny Wade is regularly called by name and her story constantly repeated.

The government's response to the 2008 financial crisis provides another illustration of the system trumping traditional values. While acknowledging that the actions of many financial institutions had caused the problems, the government found itself unable to take remedial actions due to the size

---

17. Illich, "To Honor Jacques Ellul."
18. Ellul, *The Technological Society*, 84.

of the companies. It was impossible to impose certain regulations without causing the whole economic system to fall apart. "Too big to fail" had to be accepted as a necessary characteristic of the modern technological society. Applying traditional, ethical judgments would only make the crisis worse.

Although most people easily agree that modern technology has brought great challenges to our world, many question if these are as radical as Ellul and Illich present them. The latter sometimes accuse the two scholars of being too fatalistic. They argue "too big to fail" was really a political judgment used in the financial crisis to justify not prosecuting the criminal activity of social elites.

As far back as 1986, Langdon Winner wrote extensively about government officials using technology to promote their own agendas. His classic example was the city planner Robert Moses, who consciously built low overpasses on Long Island parkways to prevent buses from using them. His goal was to prevent poor inner-city minorities who could not afford cars from using his beach parks on the island. Today we see even more sophisticated projects, such as intricate gerrymandering to secure districts for the party in power, sophisticated election strategies that target vulnerable voters, and massive monitored databases to intrude on citizens' privacy.

Others raising questions about the radical conclusions advanced by Ellul and Illich believe *technique* does not place us in a world beyond good and evil, but rather diverts and distracts our attention away from the ethical matters that impact our lives. William Shirer's picture of Albert Speer in his classic *The Rise and Fall of the Third Reich* offers a telling example. Shirer reported that Speer, Hitler's chief technician, never fully understood the consequences of his work until late in the Russian Campaign. Standing on the front lines, he saw for the first time that his cannon actually killed people. Up until then he had just performed his assigned job, working with the technology necessary to make better weapons. Casualties were simply abstractions describing the effectiveness of his work. Standing on the Western Front, he finally put his work into its existential context. The report is put into perspective when scholars give Speer credit for extending the Second World War by as many as two years.

Neil Postman attempted to address these questions when he divided the history of technology into three stages. He labeled the first a tool-using culture, in which traditional values shaped the way we used tools. He maintained that we presently live in a technocracy, where traditional and technological thought forms or worldviews live together in an uneasy tension.

The six assumptions he lists as essential to the thought-world of technology are very similar to those we have been using for *technique*.

> These include the beliefs that the primary, if not the only goal of human labor and thought is efficiency; that technical calculation is in all respects superior to human judgment; that in fact human judgment cannot be trusted, because it is plagued by laxity, ambiguity, and unnecessary complexity; that subjectivity is an obstacle to clear thinking; that what cannot be measured either does not exist or is of no value; and that the affairs of citizens are best guided and conducted by experts.[19]

Postmann believed we are rapidly headed for a third stage he designated as a technopoly, where the technological will take on totalitarian features as it eliminates all traditional values by making them "invisible and therefore irrelevant."[20] In fact, he claimed the United States was already a technopoly, so far the only one in our world.

Nevertheless, in the last chapter of his book he made an appeal for his readers to become "loving resistance fighters." Echoing President Obama's call for the liberal arts to prevent our falling into this final stage, he claimed "perhaps the most important contribution schools can make to the education of our youth is to give them a sense of coherence in their studies, a sense of purpose, meaning, and interconnectedness in what they learn."[21] Relevant to our study, he believed this curriculum should include a course in comparative religion that "would deal with religion as an expression of humanity's creativeness, as a total, integrated response to the fundamental questions about the meaning of existence."[22] He felt this might at least enable us to step back and open up a serious conversation that would allow us to critique and modify *technique*.

Conclusions

The goal of our study is twofold. The first is to discern the ways that technology has affected the church's use of the three theological virtues of faith, hope, and love. The second is to investigate if and how the church might use

---

19. Postman, *Technopoly*, 48–51.
20. Postman, *Technopoly*, 48–51.
21. Postman, *Technopoly*, 185–86.
22. Postman, *Technopoly*, 198.

the three virtues to critique *technique* and so provide guidance for society to use technology appropriately.

As Postman implied, religions intrinsically resist the reductionism on which *technique* is built. They are in a position to do this because they inherently address all things from the perspective of the whole. George Lindbeck offered a definition in his *The Nature of Doctrine: Religion and Theology in a Postliberal Age* that is widely cited by modern theologians. He described religion as "a kind of cultural and/or linguistic framework or medium that shapes the entirety of life and thought."[23] He went on to speak of religions as "comprehensive interpretative schemes, usually embodied in myths or narratives and heavily ritualized, which structure human experience and understanding of self and world."[24] Paul Tillich said much the same thing when he spoke of religion wrestling with the ultimate concerns of humanity. So did one of the most respected Lutheran scholars, Robert Jenson, who claimed that the church's message is about "everything in life," a "comprehensive unity,"[25] and the "encompassing plot of all human stories."[26]

Any attempt to reduce Christian faith to that which can be controlled or completely explained is to deny its very essence in two ways. First, it fails to look at the totality of life, and second, it denies the singularity of all persons and things. Biblical theology maintains that mystery remains after all attempts to explain anything in creation, because all is in a relationship with God who is like a whirlwind beyond human control,[27] and as wind and fire that blows and burns as it pleases.[28] A complementary assumption is that each person is a child of God who is special in their own right and that each part of creation is always new and unlike any other.

Pope Benedict XVI constantly spoke and wrote about the destructive effects of reductionism. In one of his favorite themes, he lamented the deterioration of European culture, whose former greatness he asserted was based on its Christian foundations.[29] In the past, Christianity had offered a wisdom on which Western society could base values and standards. In the

---

23. Lindbeck, *The Nature of Doctrine*, 33.
24. Lindbeck, *The Nature of Doctrine*, 32.
25. Jenson, *Story and Promise*, 1.
26. Jenson, *Story and Promise*, vii.
27. Job 38.
28. Acts 2.
29. For an example see "The Transformation of Christian Faith-Hope in the Modern Age," *Spe Salvi*, #16–23.

present there are many options, but no norms by which to evaluate them. Everything is about means, nothing about ends. Benedict usually blamed this deterioration on the West's consistent dependence on science and technology, which offer no replacement for Christian wisdom. However, he never spent much time explaining what that means. Rather he quickly turned to Nietzsche's anarchism, implying that the conflict was about doctrines rather than values and practice.

We agree with Benedict that *technique* is slowly morphing the ideals and concepts associated with Christianity. However, we are going to stay focused on the specific ways that science-based technology is currently changing everyday values and practice. Again, we agree with Postman that people need to become cognizant of what is taking place and then participate in making decisions that can use technology in a humane manner. Christians have always believed this kind of decision-making has involved the theological virtues of faith, hope, and love.

Both Ellul and Illich are helpful in our endeavor to critique and use technology appropriately because both studied the technological society from the Christian perspective. Ellul wrote extensively on both theology and sociology. Illich was a Roman Catholic priest as well as a social critic. Although he chose not to practice his ordination in an official capacity, the church never defrocked him and he never renounced his priesthood.

We shall continue our study with an examination of how Christianity in general and Christian language in particular have been affected by modern technology. We shall then look specifically at how *technique* has reshaped people's perceptions of the three theological virtues of faith, hope, and love, following that with an attempt to answer the question "so what?"

2

Christianity in the Technological Society

ON JANUARY 1, 1900, the people of North Haven, Connecticut met on the town green to welcome the twentieth century.[1] Presentations by the town's clergy were the highlight of the celebration. Each of these preachers, Congregationalist, Baptist, and Roman Catholic, gave essentially the same speech. They echoed each other's optimism, giving thanks for modern technology's promise to end humanity's basic problems. All three believed that technology would feed, clothe, and house the entire world in the next hundred years. Each used the words of their own tradition to proclaim that God was using technology to bring the kingdom of heaven to earth.

There was no way that any town in the US could have gathered their clergy in 2000 to unanimously champion the prospect of technology solving all the world's problems in the near future. The new century dawned amid apocalyptic fears that Y2K would disable every computer and crash the systems that they controlled. At midnight on December 31, 1999, people held their breath, terrified that a technical error could bring all sorts of suffering.

The church's problems with technology go far beyond what turned out to be discomfort from a temporary glitch. Today, the three church bodies that came together in North Haven no longer agree on the appropriate uses of technology. In fact, reading the newspapers or watching television could lead the public to think that the division between Christian denominations centers primarily on technological issues.

---

1. This is from a brochure in private collection that included texts of the three talks.

That these differences are deep-seated is evident when one examines the official statements on contraception made by the Roman Catholic and Lutheran churches. Both sets of statements were virtually the same until the development of a rubber safe enough to be used as birth control in the nineteenth century.[2]

After that technological innovation, the churches' positions went in increasingly opposite directions, diverging more and more with each new development. Their stands hardened with the introduction of "the pill" and morning-after solutions. In one way or another, the Roman Catholic pronouncements prohibited the use of contraception, because all sexual relationships should have the potential for producing new life. The Lutherans' statements, on the other hand, saw the new technology as a valuable tool that offered a number of benefits, particularly in allowing husbands and wives to plan their families more carefully.

This progressive separation goes far beyond this particular issue and these particular churches. Denominations disagree about abortion, *in vitro* fertilization, climate change, gun control, and a host of other controversial issues resulting from modern technology. Alliance in one area does not mean concurrence in another. Interestingly, official positions seem to mean little for lay practice. Polls show that churchgoers pretty much use technology the same way, regardless of their denominations' positions.

Technology has presented many profound issues for the church, sometimes consciously recognized and sometimes barely sensed. Nonetheless, few theologians explore the effects of technology on religion. They engage in all sorts of profound studies on the implications of science, but generally treat technology, where science really affects people, only superficially.

Technology in the Church

Some respected theologians still echo the optimism of the North Haven pastors. Leonard Sweet, for instance, calls on the church to regard technology as "a gift given by God" that enables us to hasten God's mission. He points to its potential for ending poverty.[3]

The more prevalent position encourages congregations to enhance their ministry by investing in the latest technological gadgets. This usually is promoted as a means to improve communication that keeps parishioners

---

2. Foltz, "Conception and Contraception."
3. Sweet, *Soul Tsunami*, 21.

informed and up to date on church happenings. The implication is that failure to do this will result in falling behind the rest of the church and society, leading to decreased membership.

Using Technology

In response, many congregations spend a great deal of time and money making sure that their lighting, sound, and air conditioning systems are up to date. They employ technicians to maintain a computer network, keeping them in constant contact with their members through Facebook, Twitter, and email. Hymns are projected on the walls. Sermons utilize PowerPoint illustrations. Some megachurches have even solved the problem of expanding their celebrity-based ministries by broadcasting their preachers' sermons into the pulpits of their many satellite churches.

For the most part, churches follow the lead of the technological society without any thought of the consequences. They seldom ask how these gadgets may affect the message that they are trying to proclaim. Indeed, very few sermons address the impact of technology on society at all.

The assumption seems to be that technology involves tools that can be used for good or evil, a rather naïve understanding from the perspective of our work. The Amish have a far more sophisticated comprehension of the problem even though their solution leaves a lot to be desired. Cognizant that the tools a culture employs significantly affects its lifestyle, they evaluate the appropriateness of every new technological device that comes along, asking how it will affect their families, tradition, and religion. In order to do this, they establish a separate environment in which they can control these decisions. They purposefully keep their communities small, end education at eighth grade, and engage only in rudimentary vocations, such as farming and simple trades. Above all, they give the community precedence over the individual, always ready to help one another when in need.

The challenge for the more conventional denominations is to appreciate the problems that come with a modern technological society without abandoning their responsibility to the larger community. That is going to mean developing theologies that address *technique* with enough depth to provide their members with grounds for making appropriate decisions in our technological environment.

Authorities and Power

Many who do look beyond the gadgets to the ideas see real challenges for Christianity. Albert Borgmann asserted that Christianity and technology are antagonists, "not simply opponents, but . . . forces that confront one another at the deepest level."[4] David Noble[5] and Rustum Roy[6] went even further, speaking of technology as the new religion to which society turns to solve all its problems.

Jacques Ellul used some helpful biblical categories to analyze how this takes place. He identified technology as one of the New Testament Powers, Principalities, and Authorities.[7] These are terms Paul used in several passages to describe the agencies that maintain the order of creation.[8]

Principalities, Powers, and Authorities play an essential role. God assigned them a function he declared "good" in the Genesis creation. In this spirit, Paul wrote, "Let every person be subject to the governing authorities; for there is no authority except from God, and those authorities that exist have been instituted by God."[9]

However, this goodness depends on their remaining in a proper relationship with God and the other Powers. Problems develop when any Power distorts this relationship and upsets the priorities of the hierarchy over which God presides. That Power then forces the others to submit to its domination rather than God's. John of the Revelation Apocalypse believed this had happened with the Roman Empire and, in contrast to Paul, called on the church to reject Rome's authority and "come out of her."[10]

Paul sometimes described salvation as putting these Powers back in order. In Colossians 1:15–20, he wrote of Christ:

> He is the image of the invisible God, the firstborn of all creation; for in him all things in heaven and on earth were created, things visible and invisible, whether thrones or dominions or rulers or powers—all things have been created through him and for him. He himself is before all things, and in him all things hold together

---

4. Borgmann, *Technology and the Character of Contemporary Life*, 305.
5. Noble, *The Religion of Technology*.
6. This is from multiple private conversations and public presentations by Rustum Roy.
7. Ellul, *On Freedom*.
8. Rom 8:31–39. Eph 3:7–14, 6:10–17. Col 1:15–23, 2:8–19.
9. Rom 13:1.
10. Rev 18:4.

> . . . For in him all the fullness of God was pleased to dwell, and through him God was pleased to reconcile to himself all things, whether on earth or in heaven, by making peace through the blood of his cross.

In 1 Corinthians 15:26–28, Paul made it clear that this restoration of proper order is a work in progress. Salvation will not be complete until "every ruler and every authority and power" recognizes God's supremacy. In the meantime, believers struggle to remain in a righteous relationship with God and creation. Paul confessed that even he found himself doing exactly what he did not want to do.[11]

John was saying much the same when he identified Christ as the *logos* of creation.[12] The *logos* was the reason or pattern with which God worked as he created. If he fulfilled this role, Christ restored all things to their proper order.

To call technology a Power then is not to judge it evil. Each Power plays an essential role. However, when technology creates an environment that forces all to conform to its requirements, it is operating beyond its appropriate function.

The church as an institution is also a Power that has its proper societal function. As such, it should not presume to tell the other Powers how to do their work. In fact, a perfect example of a Power gone wrong is fundamentalism, which uses the Bible as a textbook dictating scientific teaching. It is just as dysfunctional as scientism, which uses the scientific method to explain all societal issues or *technique* when it employs the technological paradigm as the only way to solve all of humanity's problems.

Ideally the Christian lifestyle respects the hierarchy in which each order of creation performs its appropriate function. Science, technology, economics, politics, entertainment, religion, and such each make their own contribution to the common good. This lifestyle offers the wisdom necessary to make technological decisions that benefit the whole society, as well as to challenge technology when it oversteps its boundaries.

Technique and Modern Christianity

Illich used colorful language to characterize the present distorted situation in which people are forced to accommodate to the needs of the technological

---

11. Rom 6:21–25.
12. John 1.

environment. He spoke of *technique* transforming human society into a Moloch system.[13] Moloch was an ancient Canaanite god who demanded child sacrifice. The Hebrews regarded this practice as an abomination ever since God's early rejection of their father Abraham's sacrifice of Isaac. Illich believed making decisions solely on the most efficient way to get what you want is a form of the child sacrifice that God abhors as it ignores the needs of future generations. Indeed, he spoke of *technique* as the very opposite of Christian values.

> This regime has given birth to a society, a civilization, a culture which, taken together, are the clear inverse of what we read in the Bible, of what is indisputably found in the text of the Torah, the Prophets, Jesus and Paul.[14]

A natural first response would be to ask why people do not see what is happening if things are so drastic. Illich's answer would be that we have difficulty discerning the great change, because *technique* is an outgrowth and subversion of Christianity.

> The unique character of the time in which we live cannot be studied rationally if one does not understand that this age is the result of a *corruptio optimi quae est pessima* (corruption of the best which turns out to be the worst) . . . . It is not possible to account for this regime if one does not understand its genesis as growing out of Christianity . . . . Among the distinctive and decisive characteristics of our age, many are incomprehensible if one does not recognize a pattern: An evangelical invitation to each person has been twisted historically into an institutionalized, standardized and managed social objective.[15]

A community proclaiming and living out the freedom of the gospel message has been transformed into an institution that has replaced spiritual gifts with techniques. The institution still employs traditional language, ritual, and doctrines even though they have assumed entirely new meanings in the technological society.

In the first chapter, we focused on how the artificial world created by the technological system breaks real-life connections. We can examine how modern technology has affected Christian thought and practices by

---

13. Illich, "To Honor Jacques Ellul."
14. Illich, "To Honor Jacques Ellul."
15. Illich, "To Honor Jacques Ellul."

examining how this disconnect with nature, place, time, and other people has taken place in the church. We are not claiming that technology is totally to blame for all the weaknesses of modern Christianity. We simply mean to show that the environment of our technological society is a major factor that is often ignored.

Breaking the Connection to Nature

Traditional Christianity regarded nature as creation and gave it a significant role in its theology. The biblical creation narratives presented God as an orator,[16] a potter,[17] and an architect.[18] As a piece of artwork reflects characteristics of the artist, so the creation reveals certain attributes of God for those who have eyes to see and ears to hear. For instance, many psalms claim that the heavens speak. Psalm 19 sings:

> The heavens are telling the glory of God; and the firmament proclaims his handiwork. Day to day pours forth speech, and night to night declares knowledge. There is no speech, nor are there words; their voice is not heard; yet their voice goes out through all the earth and their words to the end of the world.

Through the ages, most Christian theologians have assumed the psalmist's declaration that we can read God's glory, beauty, and skill in the creation. Many have also affirmed the psalmist's claim that the order of the heavens reveals that God's law is "perfect," "sure," "right," "clear," and "true."[19] Paul went so far as to claim that the creation is so saturated with meaning that humans could discern a natural moral law in it. In Romans 1:20, he wrote, "Ever since the creation of the world his eternal power and divine nature, invisible though they are, have been understood and seen through the things he has made." Modern proponents of this natural law often describe it as the grain of the universe.[20]

Jesus believed the creation also illustrated the gospel he proclaimed. It revealed a loving God who cared for the fragile lilies of the field and birds of the air. He asked his followers to ponder this lesson and thus understand

---

16. Gen 1.
17. Gen 2.
18. Ps 104. Job 38–41.
19. Ps 19.
20. Hauerwas et al., "Ethics in our time."

that God must provide for them as well.[21] In this context, creation participates in God's benevolence. It is a blessing to be used according to God's will, a gift to which humans are to respond appropriately.

This understanding is challenged in modern society that looks at the environment through the eyes of science. When it speaks of the orderliness of nature, it refers to the interrelatedness of material components from which physical laws might be derived. Science sees no meaning or purpose in this system. Any claim that nature has illuminated or clarified God's Word, inspiring humans to live according to God's will, is regarded as a subjective opinion that humans have imposed on nature.

Science-based technology believes that nature imposes limitations on humanity. It is not a gift given by God for human use but rather an environment that controls human aspirations. Technology's task is to use tools and techniques to liberate humanity so it can overcome these natural limits. When this is accomplished, nature becomes a resource that humans can use for their needs and wants.

This transformation of benevolent creation into indifferent, threatening nature has presented a challenge for Christianity. One quite appropriate response has been to address the discomfort and anxiety that has resulted from humanity's broken relationship with creation. Modern spirituality has become wellness, a means to a healthy existence that brings the body and soul back in touch with the natural rhythms of life.

This is quite different from past spirituality, whose primary goal was to establish unity with an otherworldly God. A spiritual exercise in mysticism was a path to unification with the divine that very well might destroy rather than promote physical well-being. In its worst forms these spiritual practices could bring pain and harm to the body.

For the most part, the modern church sees medieval fasting, self-denial, and austerity as misdirected superstition, not much different from self-flagellation. Today its spiritual exercises try to reestablish a healthy relationship with creation. They promote a Sabbath lifestyle whose rhythms allow time for participants to stop and ponder who they are and what they should be doing.

The most obvious exercise is the retreat that removes people from artificial urban environments and places them in rural camps and monasteries. Participants are invited to turn off the noise of machines and listen to the sounds and silence of the creation. Bible study, worship, and leisurely

---

21. Matt 6:25–34.

discussion take place in the woods, facilitating a benevolent relationship with creation.

Paradoxically, some attempts to return to the natural rhythms of life employ technological gadgets and techniques. Internet sites enable the user to remain at home while walking through virtual forests, complete with the sights and sounds of the outdoors. Most of these sites play digital recordings of bird songs or rustling leaves. A variation features a virtual walk on the beach that uses the sounds of ocean waves to calm the participant. Clearly there is a good bit of irony in the church using electronic media to retreat from the anxieties and confusions associated with the technological society.

Another exercise replaces traveling to the woods with laying out an indoor maze on the floor of a large room, perhaps by pushing back the pews in the nave. One by one, participants enter the maze, walking slowly to the first designated area, where they pause to read and ponder a selected passage. They are encouraged to take their time before proceeding to the following stops. The rationale is that the maze models the twists, turns, and dead ends we encounter as we make our way through life. By walking the maze, a person is supposedly encouraged to make contact with who they are. This exercise, like the yoga classes and other forms of meditation that are increasingly appearing in Christian congregations, fosters a mindfulness that enables participants to become more aware of their bodies and surroundings. The goal, however, is not so much discerning God's will as it is getting in touch with the "real you."

Another appropriate response is the changed understanding of natural law theory. The ancient Jewish and Christian communities that formed around biblical narratives might read a universal law reflecting the Torah in the heavens. Medieval Christendom had little trouble seeing Aristotelian logic embedded in nature. However, the modern technological society finds only indifferent physical processes offering no social lessons. In reaction, natural law theorists now base their theories on consensus rather than nature. They define natural law as those concepts on which all rational thinking persons can agree. What was once a natural concept is now a social one.

These programs are appropriate responses to science-based technology's picture of nature. They are efforts to use tradition in addressing the modern situation in which the church finds herself. They might to be modifications, but they are certainly not distortions of her message.

Those teaching the "Laws of Creation" practice a far more questionable program. They react to scientific theories that see no religious or ethical values in natural processes by claiming that the Bible reveals how things really operate. These laws are supposedly the principles that God used in his work, built into creation just like gravity. Although they were previously obscured by human sin, Christ's ministry revealed them once again. Indeed, the salvation he offers is simply the clear explication of these laws so that people can use them to gain what they seek, whether that be health of body, family, or finance.

At the time of writing this chapter, you could observe how prevalent the teaching of the "Laws of Creation" have become by tuning in on any Saturday morning to David Currillo's Inspiration Camp Meeting on the INSP network. The entire morning was filled with well-known preachers following one another each half-hour. All of them offered the five Laws of Creation in various formats

The five Laws are 1) The Law of Forgiveness, which claims that we shall not find success in life unless we forgive others as we have been forgiven, 2) The Law of Faith, which insists we can only receive what God offers when we have faith, defined as confidence rather than trust, 3) The Law of Expectation, which contends that there is no benefit from our good deeds and tithes until we have the expectation that there will be a harvest, 4) The Law of Agreement, which promises that God will grant any petition if two or three believers concur, and 5) The Law of the Seed, which discloses that the basic principle of creation is the seed, interpreted to mean that we must give God something to work with before he can give us anything in return.

Currillo's Camp Meeting might have gone the way of most Christian television programs. Our study of online churches found they regularly change formats to keep up with their followers' interests.[22] However, these laws still form the core of televangelists' preaching. If you tune in to their shows anytime during the week, you'll hear the same message. The laws have also become mainstays of evangelical preaching in local parishes. And because they reduce complex Christian teachings to short sound bites, they have infiltrated the popular theology mouthed by the laity and clergy of more traditional denominations.

Yet it is clear these laws have no connection to nature as understood by modern science. They are in no ways natural laws like gravity. As we

---

22. Foltz and Foltz, "Religion on the Internet."

shall argue at the end of the chapter, they are really techniques that operate in the virtual reality of *technique*.

Breaking the Connection to Place

Place is also essential in Christian theology. The best way to illustrate this is to begin with the importance of the body. Most biblical scholars think that both the Old and New Testaments have no concept of person apart from bodily presence. The Bible never speaks of an incarnated soul, but rather an animated body. It never refers to a soul having a body, but a body that is alive.[23]

This leads Nancey Murphy to describe the Christian understanding of the human as "nonreductive physicalism."[24] Bodily presence, often described as "real presence," is essential. "When we say that a human being is 'personally present,' as a rule we mean that this person is with us 'as a whole' in her full identity. Not merely an image, a letter, a representative, a shared conception or memory, but this human being is bodily present."[25]

This is so central to their belief that every Sunday Christians use the Apostles' Creed to profess "the resurrection of the body." The clear intent is to proclaim that the whole, complete person is resurrected. That person is identified in the resurrection as they were in their lifetime, by their physical appearance as well as their spirit. Their bodily presence is essential for their personhood. The prototype was established when the risen Jesus appeared in bodily form to his apostles, inviting them to touch him and share meals. In 1 Corinthians 15, Paul insisted that life after death is hardly real unless a person is raised with a body. There is nothing ethereal in our encounters with the divine. They all involve full contact of body, mind, and spirit.

This insistence on embodiment obviously presumes being embedded in a particular place. After describing Christ's bodily ascension into heaven, Christians still associated his presence among them with body and place. He appeared in the bread and wine of the eucharistic meal or the approach of a stranger in need. The church herself was called the body of Christ. Although they confessed the holy catholic church as a world-spanning organization, they always regarded the gathering of persons in a local congregation as her fundamental entity. Practicing the faith necessitated a place

23. McCasland, s.vv. "Man, Nature of," 243–34.
24. Murphy, "Nonreductive Physicalism," 127–48.
25. Welker, *What Happens in Holy Communion?*, 93.

where people could touch one another, pour water on one another, and share a meal.

Even the command to love your neighbor implies the importance of locality. It certainly does not mean that you only care for people nearby, but it stresses the need not to overlook them. The fullest measure of Christian love includes ministering personally to all the needs of the person before you.

Modern technology has now introduced cyberspace as if it were a place where people can meet much like they do in a neighborhood. Some futurists predict that this promises a totally mediated life that will free humanity from all limitations of space. That includes church pundits, who talk about an "emerging electronic church" that they think will become the principal means of worship in the future.

Christians do extensively and enthusiastically use the Internet for religious purposes.[26] However, very few employ it for worship. The great majority only go online to research biblical and theological topics. Most of those we polled were well aware that cyberspace is a socially contrived artificial space. Nonetheless, they thought that the local church community could benefit by increasing some forms of online ministry. These were described as extending rather than replacing the local community.

We were surprised that we did not find more associative Internet-based communities. Those we found functioned like the epistles in the early church. They shared experiences and opinions, bestowed blessings and reprimands, made requests for prayer, and provided a little teaching. Often the sites addressed controversial issues. For instance, a gay man turned to "The Ooze," an online church that identified itself as a center for "evolving spirituality," because the congregations in his small rural town did not accept him. We saw this kind of thing so often that we came to see these online communities as places where suffering or oppressed people could go to converse with others experiencing the same problems, much like many other online chat rooms. However, most online churches, like The Ooze, eventually fade away. Those that were very popular when we studied them twelve years ago are all gone now.

In contrast, television ministries featuring celebrity types are still going strong. This probably says something very important about electronic media. Associate online church communities that try to provide a ministry dealing with essential spiritual matters are bound to fail. Although

26. Foltz and Foltz, "Religion on the Internet."

The Ooze tried to compensate by offering two national conventions each year where participants could gather face-to-face, these obviously were not enough.

Televangelists, on the other hand, conform their ministries to the terms of the media and find an ongoing audience. Because sensationalism and marketing work well through electronic media, they play up miracle-working and fundraising. However, televangelists ignore the most essential Christian ministries, because they don't play well on-screen. You cannot baptize or share communion meals with those viewing you electronically. You can preach simple lessons, but you are never going to teach profound theology using the very short sound bites that work on television. Many televangelists are Pentecostals who realized a long time ago that speaking in tongues does not work on the tube. In fact, they have come to prefer reporting charismatic experiences rather than taking the viewer into their healing services.[27]

This leads Robert Jenson to assert that the church can use the Internet "to teach theology" and "to invite the world's observation"; however, "the political and technological structure of the Internet prevents the church from *fully* proclaiming the Gospel through it."[28, 29] "God loves you" comes out hollow and ineffective when spoken by someone who has no idea who you are.

Hubert Dreyfus goes further, believing that the Internet cannot be used for religious purposes at all because it undermines unconditional commitments. Without face-to-face contact, there is no vulnerability. Dreyfus thinks that cyber-experiences are similar to playing video games and watching movies. They are interesting, but because their disembodied nature eliminates risk they are little more than unreal theater.[30]

Albert Borgmann echoed this, claiming that this lack of embodiment prevents people from truly experiencing one another and therefore from holding on to reality. In *Holding on to Reality: The Nature of Technology at the Turn of the Millennium*, he writes:

> We are essentially bodily creatures that have evolved over many hundreds of thousands of years to be mindful of the world not just through our intellect or our sense but through our very muscles

---

27. Foltz and Foltz, "Religion on the Internet."
28. Jenson, "The Church and Mass Electronic Media," 161–62.
29. Italics are ours.
30. Dreyfus, *On the Internet*.

and bones. We are stunting and ignoring this ancestral attunement to reality at our peril.[31]

The Vatican addressed this disembodiment that characterizes cyberspace when it asserted that "solidarity" should be the basic principle of communication ethics. "The good of persons cannot be realized apart from the common good of the communities to which they belong."[32] "It [solidarity] is not a feeling of vague compassion and shallow distress at other people's troubles, but a firm and persevering determination to commit oneself to the common good of their communities."[33]

Breaking the Connections to the Time

Time is as critical as place in all three of the Western religions. Each recognizes a historical development in God's relationship with his people. Jews identify God by remembering his interaction with their ancestors. He is the God of Abraham, Isaac, and Jacob. Christians build upon this history of salvation by proclaiming that Jesus of Nazareth continues this interaction in a critical manner. Muslims see themselves as a further step in this historical development, accepting most parts of the Christian Old and New Testaments, but regarding Mohammed as the fulfillment of the movement.

All three of these world religions observe a Sabbath lifestyle that sets aside special times to remember their histories. Throughout most of their past, this included punctuating the day with regular periods of prayer. These periods of prayer played such an important function that medieval monks invented reliable clocks in order to mark their hours accurately.

All three Western religions also designate one day a week not only to worship, but also to rest from the tedium of work and to remember their heritage. For instance, Jews observe the Sabbath from sunset Friday to sunset Saturday in order to remember that they were once slaves in Egypt who had to work constantly in service to an imperial power. Each Sabbath they celebrate their freedom by taking a day off, which should include remembering to care compassionately for those under their authority.[34] Christians

---

31. Borgmann, *Holding on to Reality,* 220.
32. Vatican, "Ethics in Communication," #22.
33. Vatican, "Ethics in Communication," #3.
34. Deut 5:12–15.

worship on Sunday in remembrance of their Christ being resurrected on the first day of the week.

All three religions celebrate annual festivals that recall pivotal past events. Their observance includes rituals that enable participants to relive these sacred moments. The Jewish Passover remembers the Exodus when God freed her people from Egyptian slavery. The Muslim Ramadan commemorates Mohammed receiving the Koran. The church year, built around Christmas and the Holy Week-Easter events, enables Christians to participate ritually in the events that have shaped who they are.

Remembering their past is so central that religions are often described as traditions. Recalling past events that are regarded as sacred goes beyond the intellectual or emotional interest in ancestors that we associate with people searching for their families' genealogies. Tradition is regarded as wisdom from the past that shows the way for living in the present. It alleviates the need to cope afresh with each new religious experience or challenge. Canon, creed, custom, and ceremony set foundational standards for making decisions in the present.

This understanding of time is pretty much lost in a technological society. The demands of economic activities keep us from observing the daily hours. The three calls to prayer, which nowadays are usually broadcast over electronic loudspeakers, are pretty much ignored in most Muslim communities as business goes on as usual. About the only Christians who observe the hours are monks, who live in an isolated environment.

It is well near impossible for an entire community to observe a common Sabbath. Some people have to maintain our vast technological systems even while others rest. Some have to work in order to provide our present forms of recreation that center on professional sports and entertainment. Most of the population cannot even remember the Blue Laws that forced businesses to close on Sundays. Most were rescinded over fifty years ago when they became an annoyance to the functioning of a growing technological society.

Tradition is devalued in this environment. As we heard in JFK's commencement address, the wisdom of the past is regarded as an obstruction to meeting our present challenges. The past is useful primarily for passing on information and knowledge that can be used to solve technical problems. The argument is often made that technology has changed the world so rapidly that past wisdom is irrelevant.

This devaluation of tradition has brought significant changes to the modern church. It has led to an emphasis on practice rather than theology, the pragmatic rather than theoretical. Without the check of tradition, usefulness, the keystone of technology, has become the standard. Ethicists report that it has become the norm by which people evaluate their scholarship.[35] Biblical scholars claim that they are expected to read biblical passages not in terms of what the original writers meant, but rather in terms of how they are helpful for modern living.[36]

It is quite common to hear people express admiration for the practices of religions while acknowledging that they think their doctrines are silly. They like the family values of Mormonism, but are skeptical of Joseph Smith's visions. Others engage in yoga and other Buddhist exercises without any interest in the theology behind the practices. They seek the peace and awareness provided by meditation as a coping mechanism in a confusing world. Families who do not consider themselves believers send their children to church to learn the Christian values that they consider important for a successful life. However, the most telling examples might be poll after poll that reveal professing Christians practice similar lifestyles regardless of the differences in doctrine taught by their denominations. For instance, virtually the same percentages of members in all denominations use artificial contraception regardless of their church's theological position.

Many welcome highlighting practicality, which emphasizes clarity, function, and pragmatic results. They believe that it speaks to real everyday needs and distills out superstitious elements. They appreciate efforts that seek prudent ways to bring about Christianity's goals.

Another change has been the emergence of special interest theologies that emphasize how the gospel affects their specific group at the present time. The first of these was the liberation theology that became popular in Latin America beginning in the 1950s. This Roman Catholic movement used Bible study as a technique for empowering poor people. Meeting in small groups, they first discussed the parishioners' immediate needs, then searched the Scriptures for inspiration, and finally sought solutions in political action. Black, feminist, and gay and lesbian theologies followed the same format as they used the Scriptures to build self-respect and foster humanitarian action. Conservative groups accused these special interest theologies of giving preference to caring for human need rather than teaching

---

35. Hauerwas et al., "Ethics in our time."
36. Attridge, "From the Dean's Desk."

church doctrine. The Vatican suppressed both liberation theology and the women's religious movement, claiming that they placed humanitarian good works over saving souls. Often the attack contained a self-righteous *ad hominem* argument, accusing these groups of giving priority to relevance rather than faithfulness.

The danger is that ignoring tradition can lead to a customized religion that operates like word processing: picking and choosing, cutting and pasting. The most sophisticated cyber church that we examined offered the worshiper a choice of architecture, music, sermon topic, and prayer request for their online worship. Users could shape their worship to meet their current needs.

One of our friends captured the problem by penning a humorous dialogue between God and a televangelist in which God lays out his plan for salvation and the televangelist dismisses it as unmarketable.[37] God responds that this is the program, take it or leave it. The televangelist thinks about it for a while, then decides to divide the program into parts and preach only those that are marketable. The church becomes a business and its members become consumers who must be entertained into buying the product.

Stephen Ellingson finds this customization in the megachurches, which he describes as communities of interest in contrast to the mainline communities of memory.[38] These giant congregations are organized around small self-interest groups that bring together those with similar life situations. These groups study the Scriptures and traditions in terms of their own needs and interests. Ellingson observes that this redefines the faith in individual and therapeutic terms, reducing it to a set of principles that make the individual happy or satisfied. The pastor becomes a life coach or counselor. The congregation assumes many characteristics of the twelve-step programs that often meet in their classrooms. Success judged in terms of personal problem-solving is elevated above faithfulness to God and his teachings.

The examples we have cited so far reflect the more creative efforts some Christian groups have used in adjusting to the technological society. Past tradition still plays a significant function. That cannot be said of those that follow. They allow technology to corrupt the basic aspects of the faith. Succumbing to the values of *technique*, they become mired in the present moment.

37. Nordvall, personal correspondence.
38. Ellingson, *The Megachurch and the Mainline*.

Many churches make no bones about rejecting tradition. The Pentecostal churches that sprang up in the early twentieth century openly describe themselves as restorative rather than reforming. This extraordinary claim maintains that the church has been corrupted since the first century. There is no basis for the pretensions of the Roman Catholics or the Protestants that the roots of their doctrines can be traced all the way back to Jesus' apostles. It is only now in their charismatic ministries that God has restored the spiritual gifts and offices that Jesus' resurrection made possible 2,000 years ago. God speaks directly to them either through "glossolalia," often described as speaking in tongues, or by "words of knowledge" that use the vernacular.

Of course, the traditions that the Pentecostals reject include the checks necessary for evaluating personal religious experiences such as glossolalia and words of knowledge. Accountability becomes very difficult, if not impossible, if all depends upon a person receiving a message directly from God. On what grounds can you object when someone claims that God is speaking to you through him? You might question whether God threatened to kill Oral Roberts if he did not raise two million dollars for his own ministry or whether God instructed Creflo Dollar to raise millions for a private jet, but without tradition you have no foundation on which to support your feelings.

This rejection of tradition is epitomized by Scientology, which literally stands classic Christianity on its head. The influence of technology is evident in every feature.[39] It has no concept of any particular god, accepting just about any picture with its catch-all slogan "if it works for you." It advertises itself as a self-improvement program and unabashedly uses technical terms and devices. In fact, it speaks of "techniques" rather than teachings. The most obvious of these involves auditing sessions that hook adherents to E-meters, supposedly scientific devices that perform as spiritual lie detectors. They are then asked questions that are designed to reveal the lies by which they live. These lies have supposedly left "engrams," or psychic scars, that are cleared once they are recognized. Devotees progress through well-ordered steps until they become operating "thetans" who are able to control their environment. Scientology, like technology, sees its ultimate goal as overcoming natural human limitations, identified here as matter, energy, space, and time, or MEST.

---

39. Reitman, "Inside Scientology."

Technology's inclination towards commercialism is also apparent. Every program, book, and service has a price clearly marked. Evangelism becomes marketing, complete with celebrity endorsements. In 1955, Scientology founder L. Ron Hubbard began Project Celebrity, which courted superstars who could be used to sell his new religion. The most prominent effort was building extravagant Celebrity Centres in major cities, such as Los Angeles, Paris, and Nashville. The fact that most people name Tom Cruise, John Travolta, Jenna Elfman, Kirstie Alley, or Elisabeth Moss when asked to name Scientologists attests to the success of the program.

Joel Osteen, the present celebrity of the power of positive thinking school, openly acknowledges that he ignores what had once been regarded as essential parts of the tradition. He responds to questions about the absence of any prophetic content in his message by asserting the need for giving hope and encouragement in this time. He counsels his followers to look back and say "I done good!" rather than to confess their sins. His prosperity gospel believes "all things are possible with God."[40] In other words, you can achieve anything you want if you put your mind to it. You just have to use the proper techniques, such as the "expectation that gets God's attention." Note the similarity to the Laws of Creation that we examined earlier. These techniques will provide "breaks and promotions." In this context, faith is believing that you can be anything you want, not trusting that God will provide for your needs.

The power of positive thinking school has infected almost all modern religious practice. The founder of the movement, Norman Vincent Peale, made no bones about redefining faith as a technique for gaining the confidence to pursue and achieve personal goals.[41] His disciple Robert Schuller called for a modern reformation based on self-esteem rather than justification by grace through faith.[42] He removed crosses from his Crystal Cathedral because they represented old-fashioned, oppressive doctrine. Both men justified the modification of tradition by maintaining that the times called for leaving behind negative thinking. They clearly reflect how religion becomes a psychological technique in the service of success, happiness, and health when *technique* is regarded as sacred.

---

40. Osteen, *Joel Osteen Ministries*.
41. Peale, *The Power of Positive Thinking*.
42. Schuller, *Self Esteem*.

Breaking Connections with People

In some sense, the other three disconnects build to this one. Although there are many church traditions with varied definitions of Christian community, they all want to be founded on Jesus' words in Matthew 18:20, "Where two or three are gathered in my name, I am in the midst of them." The simplest interpretation of this is found in Article VII of the Augsburg Confession, Lutheranism's basic creed. "It is sufficient to have an assembly of believers gathered to proclaim the Gospel accurately and celebrate the sacraments correctly."[43] This clearly necessitates a community gathered in order to perform specific actions. It calls for at least two people: one to speak God's Word and one to hear, one to baptize and another to be baptized, two people to share a meal.

Christian community is ideally inclusive, offering hospitality to all. Paul wrote, "there is no longer Jew or Greek, there is no longer slave or free, there is no longer male and female, for all of you are one in Christ Jesus."[44] All are recognized as essential parts of the community. As Paul argued in his classic model of the body of Christ:

> The eye cannot say to the hand, "I have no need for you".... God has so arranged the body, giving the greater honor to the inferior member, that there may be no dissension within the body, but the members may have the same care for one another. If any member suffers, all suffer together with it, if one member is honored, all rejoice together with it.[45]

This definition assumes the I-Thou relationship described by Martin Buber, two whole persons fully present to one another and able to enter into an authentic dialogue.[46] Each is treated as an equal because they are deemed a child of God. This kind of relationship checks the self-absorption that characterizes the radical individualism rampant in modern society.

In technological systems, other people are part of a mass that might be helpful in solving problems. They are engaged in I-It relationships, which Buber described as treating other people simply as means to get what one wants. They can be polled with others to gain information about what is happening, but are little able to check each other's self-absorption.

---

43. Tappert, ed., *The Book of Concord*, 32.
44. Gal 3:28.
45. 1 Cor 12:21–26.
46. Buber, *I and Thou*.

Community in the technological environment is most often observed through a screen that filters out any real human interactions. For instance, until recently my "friends" on Facebook could respond to what I was doing and feeling by hitting the "like" button. Presently, the like feature offers a range of emotions, spanning from "wow" to "sad" to "haha." If users feel more involvement, they can also reply with a very brief comment. Many young people prefer using text rather than speech as a filter for their interactions. They use text messages instead of speaking on their cell phones. At least on the surface, this seems an attempt to avoid the vulnerability regarded as an essential characteristic of traditional community. (The granddaughter of the oldest author, niece of the younger, challenged this interpretation. She reported that her peers have many deep conversations through text; sometimes because they are less inhibited and can type things they might not say out loud. She suggested that the real downside of text is that it allows users to give only a sliver of their attention to the person on the other end of the conversation.)

An essential question for the technological society is whether it is possible to gather a real community on electronic social media. Robert Jenson refuses to call online groups communities. He writes:

> ... the media cannot create or foster a community. What they create and foster is precisely a mass, a collection of persons who have no common purpose ... but who contact each other, if at all, only by way of that focus.[47]

Hubert Dreyfus agreed, claiming that the web, with its vast nonhierarchical nature, cannot produce a community.[48] Caught up in limitless information without any means to bring order, the best it can yield is a mass. We shall be continually returning to an examination of electronic community throughout our work, so for now we leave the discussion with that point.

Technique as Religion

Our study has examined a number of examples that show how modern technology has affected church thought and practice. The acceptable ones carefully employ the tools and techniques of modern technology in appropriate ways to proclaim the traditional message. The questionable reduce

47. Jenson, "The Church and Mass Electronic Media," 158.
48. Dreyfus, *On the Internet*.

Christian belief and actions to techniques, presenting the mysteries of faith as manageable technological systems.

The latter succumb to the thought forms of *technique* much as creationism conforms to scientism. Scientism presents science as a worldview that answers all human questions rather than a method that efficiently analyzes the physical nature of things. Feeling threatened when scientists regard God's activity as irrelevant for their work, fundamentalists claim that the Genesis 1 creation story is a scientific text that overrides any other finding. Of course, when they do this they concede the field to scientism's claim that a scientific explanation is all that counts.

In the same fashion, the questionable theologies concede to *technique* when they reduce church teachings to techniques that supposedly come directly from God. You cannot get any more efficient than being privy to the techniques used by the designer in creating the world. However, in trying to beat *technique* at its own game, they end up playing by its rules.

They can only offer guarantees that these are techniques God makes available by concocting an artificial world that breaks essential connections to nature, time, place, and community. Sin becomes ignorance rather than willful disobedience. Salvation demands following the proper, easily defined steps. Pastors become technicians who teach secret knowledge.

Laws of Creation

The Laws of Creation teaching that we explored above is a good example. Each of the five laws reduces the mysteries of faith to manageable techniques. Those preaching them see the Bible as a source of information rather than inspiration. They read the Scriptures as revealing formulae for successful living in the present society rather than calling for repentance that leads to a community that operates according to God's will. Reaping the rewards of living the Christian life depends on complying exactly with the techniques associated with each law.

This became apparent in Kenneth Copeland's long tract "The Law of Prosperity," which he described as an explication of the Law of the Seed and the Law of Expectation. The former maintained that we must give God something with which to work before he can give us anything in return, and the latter that there is no benefit from our good deeds and tithes until we have the expectation that there will be a harvest. Copeland used his father as an example of how these techniques demand precise compliance.

He claimed our good works establish a bank account in heaven that can be used if, and only if, we claim it. His father had tithed but remained poor throughout his life, because he never understood that he needed to claim his deposit. It was waiting for him, but he missed an essential step in the process. The laws do not work unless you fulfill every requirement.[49]

It is evident that the relationship between God and his people is reduced into a business transaction by Copeland and his ilk. The biblical covenant becomes a contract. Good health, strong family, financial success, and anything else you desire is available if you carefully and completely fulfill the terms. Richard Roberts makes this clear when he sends out signed contracts as part of the deal in all his ministries. The one he uses for the Law of Agreement reads, "When I receive your prayer request, I will hold your name and needs in my hands and pray."[50] Remember, the Law of Agreement promises that God will grant any petition if two or three believers concur. Roberts enters into a contract, making him the second partner that will guarantee success.

No wonder these kinds of ministry are fond of proclaiming that you can expect your miracle. A miracle is no longer a mighty, unexpected act from a God beyond human control and not subject to any Power, Principality, or Authority. It is simply the natural consequence of following the proper steps in an automatic process that guarantees God's compliance.

It is most important from the perspective of our study to perceive that these Laws of Creation are not based on nature as comprehended by scientific thought or creation as understood by religious teaching. They are rather techniques, conceived to be operating in a virtual reality concocted from the thought forms of *technique*.

Plan for Salvation

Another popular teaching that succumbs to *technique* is "The Plan for Salvation" that is almost always associated with The Laws of Creation. The plan is based on Bill Bright's four spiritual laws, which employ specific techniques for entering a personal relationship with Jesus.

The four laws are 1) God loves you and has a plan for your life, 2) The sin of every one of us has separated us from God and knowledge of this plan, 3) God has sent Jesus Christ as the only way we can experience his

49. Copeland, *Kenneth Copeland Ministries*.
50. Roberts, *Oral Roberts Ministries*.

love and know the plan, and 4) We must individually receive Jesus Christ as Savior and Lord if we are to experience God's love and know his plan for each of our lives.

Many of us came to know these laws when a member of the Campus Crusade for Christ read a slick pamphlet with us as an invitation to make a decision for Christ. The pamphlet, like most technical works, included diagrams that further reduced Christian proclamation into cartoon-like images.[51] Campus Crusade's plan employed four simple techniques: read the four laws, examine your life in light of these laws, accept Christ's invitation as presented in the laws, and enact your acceptance by saying a prayer like the one suggested in the pamphlet.

Richard Roberts's website makes clear that the plan depends on precisely following proper techniques. A link entitled "If You Need to be Saved, Do These Things" lays out four steps. Step 1: Come to Jesus, Step 2: Repent of your sins, Step 3: Believe in God and His Word, and Step 4: Confess in the name of Jesus. After completing these steps, the site invites the user to say a prayer of salvation and follows that with this assurance: "If you have gone through the four steps to receive Jesus Christ as your Savior and Lord, you are now born-again, ready to begin your new life in Christ. Christ saves you and keeps you saved, but now it's time for your part—to build your life around your Savior."[52]

At first the plan might seem to be simply a refinement of the methods practiced in old-time revivals, but upon closer examination you'll realize it has lost connection with Christian tradition and community. Salvation is not a free gift bestowed by God, but rather the result of following clearly defined steps. Faith is no longer trust in the unconditional love of God, but instead confidence that these techniques will work.

The model is an automated machine, in which you place money in a slot and a product comes out. Or, better yet, a computer that operates for you if you have the requisite data. Knowing the technique on which fulfillment of the law depends is more important than knowing God. Nonetheless, those who attend most evangelical churches hear some version of these techniques preached every week. Even sermons in more traditional congregations often implicitly infer the idea, "If you do this, then God will do that."

---

51. Campus Crusade, "How to Know God."
52. Roberts, "Salvation."

Conclusion

The pastors speaking at North Haven's welcoming celebration for the twentieth century believed that modern technology was ushering in the long-anticipated kingdom of God. They assumed that it would provide the means to solve humanity's basic problems and that society would instinctively use it for the common good.

Few people make that assumption in our time. The question has become, "How can we use the great power of technology appropriately?" This might be asking anything from, "How do we prevent people from using it for destructive purposes?" to, "How can we inspire people to utilize it for tackling societal problems, rather than producing gadgets for the masses and privileges for the elite?"

Like the rest of responsible society, the church should be asking how she might use modern technology with wisdom and compassion. The question again covers many concerns, which range from how she can utilize it for her mission to how she can prevent it from corrupting her message.

Our thesis is that answering these questions intelligently is based on recognizing technology's characteristics and limitations. We have been arguing that this begins by understanding how technology creates an environment that controls our decisions and actions by forcing everything to fit its requirements. That project includes examining how *technique* has changed the meaning of traditional words and concepts, including those the church has used to proclaim her message.

We also believe that appreciating the basic Christian message can lead to using technology creatively. By nature, that message resists the dominance of technological thought forms by proclaiming the fullness of life and the uniqueness of every part. It enables us to keep contact with reality by correcting any kind of reductionism that removes things from the context of nature, place, time, and community.

3

Words and Meaning

In *The Humiliation of the Word*, Jacques Ellul discussed what he regarded as the root of the problem that we've outlined in the first two chapters.

> This, then, is our situation today: through the eruption of unlimited artificial images we have reduced truth to the order of reality and banished the shy and fleeting expression of truth. Strangest of all, we are not dealing with the identification of truth with reality already found in science. Instead, this "reality" is really fiction—literally simulated, depicted. This reality is falsified, but it constitutes the new visible human universe. It is a visible universe of proliferating images produced by all sorts of techniques. No longer are we surrounded by fields, woods, and rivers, but by signs, signals, billboards, screens, labels, and trademarks: this is our universe. And when the screen shows us a living reality, such as people's faces or other countries, this is still a fiction: it is constructed and recombined reality.[1]

Ellul made quite a radical statement. He contended that *technique* takes a step backwards in humanity's search for truth. Although it claims to be scientifically based, it has placed us in an artificial world. This is not immediately apparent because it employs the images, numbers, and formulae of scientific analysis, but it does so in a manner that loses contact with the real world that science investigates. We are so enclosed on all sides by this simulated world that we have come to regard it as the real one. In the first chapter of *The Whale and the Reactor*, Langdon Winner reports that astronaut John Glenn found the actual experience of space flight less real than

---

1. Ellul, *The Humiliation of the Word*, 228.

the simulations he had experienced prior to launch. The first American to orbit the Earth mused that the synthetic laboratory representation seemed more authentic than the genuine flight. Fiction surpassed reality.

Technology and Words

Understanding Ellul's contention demands a cursory look at language's function. Thinkers have long appreciated the significance of speech, some believing it even distinguishes our humanity. Today we realize that whales, dolphins, apes, and even bees are able to convey messages to one another, but we also understand that they don't come close to the sophisticated human communication that extends across the globe and on to future generations.

Words

One of the basic human challenges is to create common sense from the data and facts that constantly bombard us. If you compare sense stimuli to kaleidoscopes or pointillist paintings, then you could say that our brains order and reassemble the color splashes and dots. Recent findings in cognitive science indicate that this process used by the brain resembles language more than machine. Like the development that takes place in a conversation, the brain judiciously selects which data it will use rather than proceeding in a mechanical cause and effect manner.

Words make order from chaos as they identify, rearrange, and analyze experience. They go beyond gestures, facial expressions, pictures, touches, pauses, melodies, and the many other ways that we point and share to name and shape. To name with a word is to create something new, to modify the world in which we find ourselves. Cognitive scientist Stephen Pinker sees evidence of this when he observes that learning every new word physically changes our brains.[2]

One of the things that words create is meaning. When we use words such as *beautiful* or *love*, we do more than point. When we string words together in sentences and narratives we go even further. Narratives create the meaningful order that we think we perceive in nature. Noam Chomsky claims that virtually every sentence is a brand-new configuration of words

---

2. Pinker, *The Stuff of Thought*, 9.

appearing for the first time.³ Each is original and brings something new into reality. Each sentence spoken in a conversation shapes the hearer, who in response speaks and shapes the previous speaker.

When Ellul claimed that language is humiliated in the modern technological society, he especially pointed to how words are removed from their existential context, the specifics of their environment, and the traditions that have filled them with meaning.⁴ Words are replaced with images because people think that this leads to objectivity. However, this is just another instance of *technique* disconnecting people.

It is true that images, numbers, and formulae might make for accuracy and precision in studying the material world, but words are necessary for human relationships and history, which are constantly changing. We might use formulae to search for truth in the research laboratory, but we usually turn to narrative in everyday life. When asked who we are, we seldom respond by listing the chemical elements and genetic components that make up our human body. Instead, we tell the stories associated with that body. We might begin with a name, but then continue with stories that involve what we have done and what we plan to do. Again, when asked to define human nature, we remember the stories of the communities in which we have lived. In an effort to grasp the coherence that we believe to be beneath all experience, we write histories. These become living traditions that go on even while always being tested by our new experiences.

Humanity's ongoing search for truth involves conversation about meaning even more than it does analysis of facts and data. Because every moment in history is unique, no word or narrative ever completes the task. So Ellul contended that the search depends upon the "blessed uncertainty of language," the ambiguity necessary for dealing with the singularity of real life.⁵ Down through the ages, many great thinkers have taught the same lesson when they claim that difference is as important as sameness when trying to accurately express truth. Augustine wrote that the beauty of the universe is made more brilliant by the opposition of contraries.⁶ Nicholas of Cusa, a mystic, found truth in the "learned ignorance" beyond contradictory statements.⁷ Truth can involve "yes" or "no," but also "yes and no."

---

3. Chomsky, *On Language*.
4. Ellul, *The Humiliation of the Word*.
5. Ellul, *The Humiliation of the Word*.
6. Augustine, *Confessions*.
7. Nicholas of Cusa, *Selected Spiritual Writings*.

Words and Meaning

Three Stages

The situation that Ellul described is only the last of many changes that the continuous development of technology has made on language. Scholars usually speak of three periods: the oral, the textual, and the electronic. We can better understand Ellul's argument if we review these. Each stage has its advantages and disadvantages, its gains and losses. As technologies have overcome the limitations of time and space, they have enabled us to communicate instantaneously with people on the other side of the planet. However, this has come at the cost of losing the richness of face-to-face conversation. In some sense, each stage has brought a narrower band of communication, which makes expressing emotions, intentions, and profound thoughts more difficult.

In the oral stage, everything was context. Most people spent their entire lives living in one locality among their extended families and close friends. Almost all communication was face-to-face, using words but also intonation, inflection, gesture, and expression. The world was very present. People thought as they spoke. Meaning was found in storytelling. People repeated narratives over and over again to understand who they were, what they believed, and what they were to do. Myth and ritual created order and continuity, but mystery remained.

Great changes took place as language was transcribed. Even though this culminated in the sixteenth century, with the invention of the printing press, most people at the time still lived in an oral world. They heard the words as they were read by the learned. Those readers even spoke the words aloud when they read in private. Illich described reading at this time as an oral practice, the act of speaking and then listening to your own words.[8]

Of course, the written word allowed writers to communicate with many more readers, even many that they would never meet face-to-face. This came at the cost of losing the intonation, inflection, gesture, and expression that allowed them to be more explicit about what they wanted to say. In the field of communication, they would say that communication became less rich.

Nonetheless, the printing press opened up new possibilities. Now people could engage in more profound thought. They could pick up a book and put it down as they pleased. They could think while and after they wrote or read. They could pause to contemplate, reflecting and making choices

---

8. Illich, "To Honor Jacques Ellul," 51–65.

about how they would interpret the words. They now had the tools for a higher level of abstract analysis and study. They could search for meaning in libraries.

The hard copy of text encouraged the setting of standards. Scholars sought the real meaning of a book, asking about the author's intentions. They spoke of authorized versions and canons. Secular society had the works of Shakespeare and the church had her Bible. In this situation, the institutional church defined its role as passing on the sacred texts of their faith to future generations. Christians had always claimed that their tradition went all the way back to the teachings of the apostles who walked with Jesus. Now they identified that tradition primarily with biblical texts.

The electronic media of the third period brought new changes that began in the nineteenth century with the telegraph and only recently became predominant with the Internet. Parents can digitally track the whereabouts of their children. Friends can constantly alert each other to what they are doing and feeling. Corporate executives can lead online committee meetings with people participating from all around the globe. Scholars can engage in extended two-way conversations that allow them to communicate much faster than traditional written letters while also stopping to contemplate what has been said before replying. Students can conduct research from their homes without searching through books in a library, instead analyzing vast amounts of information at great speed. All of this is done instantaneously, at the push of a button.

However, the gains in speed, immediacy, and abundance come with the loss of the personal contact found in the oral stage and the profundity found in the textual stage. Without face-to-face communication, those using electronic media can easily disguise their feelings, motives, and purposes. Teenagers can use their cell phones to text rather than speak with their parents in order to avoid the vulnerability of direct conversation. Facebook friends are able to cloak what they are really feeling or doing, even establishing false identities. Business people might enter into huge economic projects with partners of unknown moral character. Students must wrestle with vast quantities of information, often without the means to determine which is genuine scholarship and which is contrived research.

Far more crucial, the abundance of material and the unrestricted nature of electronic media bring intrinsic problems for profound thought. Profundity is the kind of thinking required for handling difficult societal issues that go deeper than surface, everyday concerns and longer than short-term problems. Its first task is to accumulate sufficient information. Obviously, electronic media enable immediate access to lots of data, so much that the sheer volume becomes the problem.

It is extremely difficult to manage all the information that the computer is able to supply. When using books, scholars can take the time to ponder lengthy arguments. After knowing the available facts, they attempt to sort and prioritize the issues, often applying standards established from past experience. After further deliberation, they make conclusions and decisions that are accountable. To do this well requires a considerable amount of time.

The conditions created by the profusion of data in the electronic stage challenge lengthy deliberation. The volume and fluidity of electronic media prompts an appetite for the latest and most popular. Websites must be constantly updated in order to remain relevant. If they fail to reach an audience, they can be deleted at the touch of a button. It is hard to establish authorized versions when you cannot even find original texts. Without some accepted authorities and standards, it becomes extremely difficult to evaluate and prioritize.

This is exacerbated by the narrowband automated nature of electronic communication. Facebook accommodates only short and limited comments. Tweets are made up of no more than 280 characters. Emails favor short messages. Television has reduced its average sound bite to nine seconds and changes its scenes at least every four minutes. The character of the media favors practicable short-term thinking.

This constantly changing abundance of data has altered everything about the way we use language. One clear example is that it has made alphabetized lists archaic. People now turn to Google on their home computers rather than the card catalogue in the library across town. Google's search engine produces results based on what its database estimates the user wants. At the same time, it introduces a commercial feature that tends to be associated with modern technological ventures. Clients pay to have their product appear higher on the search list. The problems associated with volume are now further complicated by special interests.

In this milieu, people take for granted that the information with which they are working has already been tampered. In many cases they welcome this. Bombarded by overwhelming amounts of data, they appreciate others sorting it out for them. For instance, newspapers are becoming obsolete, because those who once read them for balanced reports increasingly use news services that email select articles every day. These services cull the news for articles that suit the political positions of their clients. So much for hearing both sides of an argument!

The situation already has brought physical changes to our brains. In *The Shallows*, Nicholas Carr reported that the area that processes new data has enlarged to cope with the excessive amount of information constantly battering us. At the same time, the one that stores proven information has shrunk. Carr worried that these changes might lead to more difficulty engaging in deep thought and higher emotions, as both of these depend on neural processes that are inherently slow. They require a calm and attentive mind. Carr warned that these changes might affect not only our ability for profound thought and compassion, but even our physical health. After all, contemplation and meditation are natural means to overcome stress that are far more effective than drugs. His findings can help explain why bumper stickers have become more powerful motivators than eloquent essays.

Ellul and Illich believed that the electronic age had also led to a crisis of language that Ellul called the humiliation of the word[9] and Illich deemed the death of words.[10] One symptom of this critical situation is the underutilization of words. Paul Kropp reported that there are almost half a million words in the English language, but a third of all writing is made up of only twenty-two different ones.[11]

Ellul believed that the crisis goes far beyond using fewer words poorly, that it is actually centered on replacing words with images in a misguided attempt for clarity. Supposing images, pictures, and formulae more efficiently communicate reality, technicians turn to them rather than words. It is true that a picture might be worth a thousand words when it comes to depicting and analyzing things and events, but a picture is only a snapshot, pure present and nowness. It offers an image of the external world, conveying what we see rather than what we think. In a sense, an image is unprocessed sense data to which the response is the binary "yes" or "no," "like" or "dislike."

Ellul warned that images only seem efficient and accurate when used in the virtual reality of the artificial technological system. Real life is far too mysterious and singular to be captured in a snapshot. Pictures, images, and formulae might work for information sharing, but not for interpretation. For the most part they just point, while words make connections. Only the

9. Ellul, *The Humiliation of the Word.*
10. Illich, "To Honor Jacques Ellul."
11. Kropp, *The Reading Solution.*

ambiguous nature of words does justice to reality. When used properly they are the stuff of the wisdom necessary for evaluating and prioritizing the vast amount of information available to us. Words empower the profound thought necessary for making decisions about deep, long-term issues.

Plastic Words

A number of scholars have addressed this crisis of language brought about in the electronic age. An examination of their work offers helpful insights for understanding the serious situation of which Ellul spoke.

George Orwell introduced the idea of "newspeak" in his novel *1984*. This is a fictional language created by the authorities to keep the public under their control. They understand that ideas have power and that words connect us to ideas. Newspeak removed any words that might promote freedom, rebellion, or alternative thinking, replacing them with those without any shades of meaning. This left only simple dichotomies, such as pleasure and pain, happiness and sadness, goodthink and crimethink. In doing this, newspeak limited the ability of the masses to think and react in ways that the authority deemed dangerous to the establishment.

Orwell's novel resonates with us when we remember how the Nazis redefined and invented words to disguise the immoral nature of what they were doing. We, also, recognize that our own government has recently done the same with concepts such as "enhanced interrogation," "collateral damage," "unlawful combatants," "security detainees," and, increasingly, "credible evidence." These are always justified as attempts to be as accurate as possible, but it does not take long to see that they are removing words from their real contexts to prevent us from discussing what is really happening. "Enhanced interrogation" seems to be police questioning stepped up a bit to protect many good people from a few bad ones, not inflicting unbearable pain on a living human being, the kind of torture that used to appear at the beginning of ethics textbooks as an activity that all civilized people could agree was evil. "Collateral damage" sounds like an ethically justified practice rather than the bombing of innocent children. Why would anyone suspect that "deficit spending" might be a term invented by the financial community to show that the present financial crisis was caused by government spending? Or that the "trickle down" theory was invented by the wealthy to justify economic practices that have continually widened the gap between the rich and poor since 1972?

Ellul believed that the managed control of newspeak was no longer the greatest threat to language. With some effort, we can discern how some humans shape words to control other people and respond with caution and efforts to correct the situation. When the modern technological society succumbs to *technique*, however, it changes the nature of words in far subtler, hardly detectable ways.[12] Rather than humans using words to shape and give meaning to their environment, now the artificial environment of *technique* shapes words and their users to fit the system.

Ellul spoke of "commonplaces" assumed in the environment created by technology.[13] He felt that these were far more dangerous than newspeak, because they are truisms that reflect that which is taken for granted in a society. There is no need for governments or corporation to control and manage them, because they are the assumptions underlying *technique*. Unlike cultural wisdom that informs and inspires, they stimulate compliance to the global technological system. They consistently trump traditional cultural teachings. Here are a few of the thirty-three "commonplaces" that Ellul lists: "You can't act without getting your hands dirty," "The main thing is to be sincere with yourself," "Modern man has come of age," "Nobody can help anybody else," "Freedom is obeying necessity," "The machine is a neutral object and man is its master," "No more words, give us action," "Work is freedom," "Women find their freedom through work," "The spiritual side of life cannot be developed until the standard of living is raised," and "You can change anything to suit yourself." As these slogans replace the myths and narratives of our culture, they come to serve as wisdom.

Uwe Poerksen examined the "plastic words" used extensively in this technological environment.[14] These are all-purpose words that mean nothing in particular. They can be used just about anywhere because, like newspeak, they have no connection to the real world. Like plastic Lego blocks, they are combinable and interchangeable.

These plastic words interpret history as if it were nature. They reduce a gigantic area to a common denominator, dispensing with questions of good or evil. Experts love to use plastic words when explaining their projects because they sound scientific and therefore must be important and accurate. People think that only these experts can deal with such words because they themselves have no idea what they mean. They feel that they have to adjust

---

12. Ellul, *The Humiliation of the Word*.
13. Ellul, *A Critique of the New Commonplaces*.
14. Poerksen, *Plastic Words*.

to these words rather than vice versa, a good example of technology acting as a biblical power that dominates rather than serves humanity.

Nonetheless, even while pointing out that these hollow words have no content, we find ourselves using them. We constantly resort to words such as "education," "identity," "living standard," "modernization," "planning," "progress," "relationship," "value," "welfare," "basic need," "care," and "development" because they serve our purposes. We can read into them anything we please, especially our own prejudices.

Ivan Illich enjoyed playing around with plastic words, amusingly speaking a language that he called "uniquack."[15] It closely resembled the technobabble that abounds in bureaucracies and other authoritarian groups. Illich would throw out contradictory words that said nothing specific but suggested all kinds of modern shenanigans, words such as "professional friend," "needs creator," "self-accredited elite," "sick-making medicine," "impoverishing wealth," "crime-making prisons," "disabling professions," and "care consumers."

None of the four perversions of language discussed above use words to express or search for truth. Rather than attempting to make common sense of the experience impacting us, they use words to manipulate people by conjuring up images that have no connection with the real world.

Henry Frankfurt highlighted this feature in *On Bullshit,* in which he claimed that technology had turned language into "bullshit," a technique for the speaker or writer to get what they want or need. The aim of bullshitters is to impress and persuade their audience, to use language to get their own way. Frankfurt says that this can hardly be called lying, because liars deliberately make false claims. Liars know the truth, but conceal it. Bullshitters, on the other hand, are not interested in the truth at all. They seek solely to advance their own agendas. Frankfurt claimed that in this sense, bullshitters are greater enemies of the truth than liars.

Advertising is obviously the epitome of "bullshit" as it manipulates the trust between word and world, replacing substance with image to elicit an emotional response. You get an idea of how much and how fast language has changed by remembering that college students in the 1950s used to debate whether advertising was ethical. Now we are so overcome by bullshit that such debates seem trite. We pay people more money to manipulate language than to use it to seek truth.

15. Illich and Sanders, *ABC.*

Bullshit might be the culmination of the dangerous trend that Neil Postman identified many years ago with his observation that technology makes all information into entertainment.[16] Now we have the Gene Becks and the Rush Limbaughs, wordsmiths who demand that we treat them as entertainers rather than newscasters or commentators. They need only to please their audiences and sell products. There are no standards to which they are held accountable. Unable to critique what they say, we are expected only to "like" or "dislike."

The electronic age has severely damaged the trust on which language depends. In previous ages, words expressed the meaning that our culture placed on the proliferation of data that assaults us constantly. We trusted that others were using words honestly in the same way that we were. We became angry and frustrated when we felt our trust was betrayed. In *My Fair Lady*, Eliza Doolittle sang, "Words! Words! Words! I'm so sick of words!" when the words spoken around her did not correspond to the actions of those speaking them.[17] So too we trusted that words established a common sense and shared understanding. If that trust breaks down, chaos and anxiety descend upon us. When Polonius asked Hamlet what he was reading, he responded with the same, "Words, words, words," complaining that the written word that used to provide meaning in his world was now useless.[18] All appeared madness after his discovery that his uncle had murdered his father and married his mother.

Before the electronic stage, people presumed that they were usually dealing with a realistic narrative. They assumed that their words corresponded in critical ways with the real world they shared with others. Now people no longer naturally make that assumption. In the technological society, they are reduced to studying what people say, making no pretensions about having standards of truth by which to judge those words true or false. To put it another way, if you accept Frankfurt's position, the social sciences now simply analyze the way we bullshit.

Christianity and Words

All of this has profound consequences for the church. The soundness of language is crucial for Christianity. At the end of the fourth century, Augustine

---

16. Postman, *Amusing Ourselves to Death*.
17. Lerner and Loewe, *My Fair Lady*.
18. Shakespeare, *Hamlet*, II.ii.192.

wrote that God created time and space to make room for humans to engage in the conversation between the persons of the Trinity.[19] That understanding is evident in the comment that Robert Jenson made on Martin Luther's explanation to the First Article of the Creed.

> God, according to all the Scriptures, is above all the great Speaker; he is his own Word, and never relates to others by mere force, but always by personal address. That he creates something new means that he expands the field of his conversation . . . . That he creates, means that Father, Son and Spirit among themselves mention others than themselves: they speak together of . . . the great sea beasts, and so there are the great sea beasts for them to discuss. God converses the world into being.[20]

Luther's contemporary, the great humanist Erasmus, expressed the same idea when he translated the prologue to John's gospel as "In the beginning there was Speech (rather than "the Word"); that Speech was in the beginning with God, and everything God made, he made by speaking."[21]

Although these thoughts are seldom expressed or discussed in most parish churches, much less in universities or even seminaries, they find tremendous support in Scripture. Throughout both the Christian Old and New Testaments, God related to the world and people primarily through speech. This is so prominent that the Word of God is used to express God's presence.

Word and Creation

In the first chapter of Genesis, the best-known creation story, God speaks all things into existence. It seems obvious that we are reading a poetic narrative that appreciates Ellul's "blessed uncertainty of language." Both the meaning and the mystery of God's creation are maintained by the ambiguity of words. Fundamentalists distort this when they treat the creation story as a scientific explanation. For that matter, anyone who pretends that seven days might mean seven eons also misses the point. Even the accomplished scientist Francis Collins didn't get it when he described the genome code

---

19. Augustine, *Confessions*, 277.
20. Jenson, *A Large Catechism*, 21–22.
21. A lengthy discussion can be found in Von-Wedel, *Erasmus of Rotterdam*, 133–44.

as God's language, implying that this scientific analysis of reality is also the secret to its truth and meaning.²²

In this poetic narrative, God uttered, "Let there be . . ." and "it was so." His word gave order to chaos. His naming gave identity to each part. Every time God speaks he creates something new, forming the world and shaping lives. When humans are included in the naming, we are offered a clue as to what being created in God's image means. Speech defines the uniqueness of the divine and the human.

Janet Soskice came to that conclusion in a recent *Christian Century* article when she wrote:

> The early chapters of Genesis present God as a speaking being. God is throughout presented as summoning, calling, admonishing, commanding, and creating by his word. This imagery is recurrent in the Hebrew Bible and the New Testament. We might say that the Genesis image of God is of a God of creative address. What might it mean, then, to consider that it is as "speaking beings" that we are in the image of God?²³

According to Genesis, the creation opens an ongoing conversation that characterizes the divine-human relationship. It pictures an intimate face-to-face conversation, taking place in a garden in the cool of the evening. Even animals participate in this paradise.

Genesis uses four myths to explain how this conversation has been disrupted. The best known is a discourse in the third chapter between the humans and a serpent, in which Adam and Eve are led to take the actions that break their relationship with God. The consequence is living apart from him, making face-to-face dialogue impossible.

The myth most relevant to our task is that of the Tower of Babel in Genesis 11. It attributes the diversity of languages throughout the world to humanity's use of technology for competition among themselves rather than for following God's will. The inhabitants of the city build a tower to make a name for themselves instead of using the works of their hands to serve God's community. The confusion of languages is the epitome of falling back into chaos. Neglecting God's authority destroys the order of creation. Now humans are not even able to communicate with each other, much less with God.

---

22. Collins, *The Language Of God*.
23. Soskice, "Speech bearers."

Words and Meaning

Word as Salvation

The Scriptures describe salvation as reopening this divine-human conversation, which will in turn facilitate humans creatively communicating with one another. The opening act features God coming to speak with Abraham and his wife Sarah. The blessed ambiguity is maintained in the magnificent interchange that takes place in Genesis 18 as the text pictures Abraham and Sarah speaking at various times with three men, three angels, and God himself. Both the divine and the human express themselves fully in the back and forth conversation. God promises to bless their children so that they can bless all the other families of the earth. In other words, he commits to continuing the conversation.

The Bible describes the implementation of this promise as an ongoing discourse. During periods of difficulty, God's people ask why he remains silent. When God demands repentance, he asks them to "come to him with words."[24]

The main event of the Old Testament begins with God responding to the cries of Abraham's descendants by engaging in conversation with Moses. Exodus 3 and 4 record a colorful dialogue in which both parties speak their minds freely. In the end God sends Moses to be his spokesperson, first with the pharaoh who has enslaved his people and then with the people themselves. This conversation continues as God gives Moses instructions for leading the Hebrews to freedom, dictates the Torah law, and finally relays tactics for invading the promised land. Throughout this ongoing exchange, Moses voices his opinions freely, sometimes openly disagreeing with God and sometimes even changing God's mind.

The Torah law, which might better be described as teaching, reveals a lifestyle that enables the divine-human conversation to continue. Prominent among these teachings is the commandment prohibiting the making of graven images. Although the interpretations usually go no further than reading it as prohibiting idol worship, the underlying rationale echoes the same warning about technology heard in the Tower of Babel myth. That reasoning is evident in Exodus 20:22–25:

> The Lord said to Moses: Thus you shall say to the Israelites: "You have seen for yourselves that I spoke with you from heaven. You shall not make gods of silver alongside me, nor shall you make for yourselves gods of gold. You need make for me only an altar of

---

24. Hos 14:2.

earth and sacrifice on it your burnt-offerings and your offerings of well-being, your sheep and your oxen; in every place where I cause my name to be remembered I will come to you and bless you. But if you make for me an altar of stone, do not build it of hewn stones; for if you use a chisel upon it you profane it.

The only way to relate to the living God is through words. Graven images are deaf and dumb. Not only is it impossible to visualize the deity, anything even approaching the attempt could turn into an idol. Once you begin even etching stones in the place of worship, you open yourselves up to the problem of Babel. You begin competing among yourselves over who makes a better etching, rather than concentrating on what God is saying.

The New Testament presents a further development in this redemptive conversation when it claims that God speaks through the words and actions of the man Jesus of Nazareth. The Gospel of John described him as the embodied Word of God who "lived among us" as a human being.[25] The evangelist was clearly placing Jesus in the continuity of an ongoing conversation by identifying him with the Word spoken at creation.

In the book of Acts, Jesus' ministry is presented as bringing a new period of clarity to the conversation. The Pentecost story in the second chapter illustrated the resolution of Babel's confusion of language. People who shared Jesus' Holy Spirit could once again understand God and each other, no matter what their language. Just about every biblical vision of the future maintains this characteristic of salvation by featuring God speaking face-to-face with his people.

Christian Language in the Three Stages of Technological Change

If God is a speaker whose relationship with his people can best be described as a conversation, and if the image of God that identifies humanity is speech, then the changes that technology has wrought on language are critical. We can trace these by revisiting the oral, textual, and electronic stages.

The Oral Word

The Christian life is founded on experiences and eyewitness reports from the oral period. The testimonies and the narratives that formed around

---

25. John 1:14.

them became part of an oral tradition that was passed on through storytelling and ritual. Paul referred to this oral tradition in 1 Corinthians. In the fifteenth chapter, he introduced a list of those who had experienced Jesus after his resurrection with the words, "I handed on to you as of first importance what I in turn had received." In the eleventh, he began an account of Jesus' Last Supper with, "I received from the Lord what I passed on to you." At this stage, becoming Jesus' follower meant trusting people and believing their reports.

As in all personal encounters and conversation, there is always incompleteness and mystery. Those engaged strain to explain what they mean and struggle to understand what the others are saying. Ambiguity is taken for granted. Clarity is sought in the back and forth of conversation.

Jesus demonstrated this ambiguity by refusing to offer rigid and final definitions. For instance, when asked to define the kingdom of God, he always responded with a parable rather than a precise analysis. These stories begin with, "The kingdom of God is something like . . ." However, the story that follows is not presented as a final statement. Soon afterwards he offers another parable, introduced more or less with, "On the other hand, it is also something like . . ." It appears that his hearers understood this ambiguity, as the same stories are given various meanings in different Gospels. People seemed to have passed on these stories feeling free to add their own take in the telling. Each person heard the words in the context of their own situation.

The Written Word

Text gained importance as the culture slowly moved to the next stage. The written text facilitated Christian contemplation and deep thought. It also limited the charismatic enthusiasm of the oral period. Believers now dealt more and more with secondhand experience. Charisma, enthusiasm, and prophecy were mediated through written words and narratives.

The church became more interested in stability and order than creativity and prophecy. Although anyone reading the Bible easily detects different opinions and conflicting traditions, the hierarchy searched for the authentic one. Often this involved claiming the power to authorize one tradition over another. In the oral stage, clergy and community were the primary means used to check experience. Now canon, creed, ceremony, and custom gained importance. As the church came to rely on written texts rather than fluid story, the canon took a special place in testing what claimed to be God's Word. Indeed, many Reformation leaders acted like the written word was the only worthy standard.

Still, the church retained the priority of the dynamic spoken word. She made Christ present by remembering him with words. Her liturgy was conversational, narrative, and antiphonal. Even the sacraments demanded words. Luther wrote, "Water by itself is only water, but with the Word of God it is a life-giving water which by grace gives new birth through the Holy Spirit."[26] All of these assume that the words must be spoken face-to-face, not written or transmitted electronically, if their full power is to be experienced. The proclamations "God loves you" and "God forgives you" only carry their full impact if made in the context of a real living human relationship in which the speaker might be rejected.

The Electronic Word

Like the rest of society, Christianity benefits from the gains in speed, immediacy, and abundance that come with this stage. On the other hand, it is also hit harder than most other communities by the loss of personal contact found in the oral stage and profundity in the textual stage. Both of these are essential to the church's message and mission.

The church by nature deals with the ultimate questions and basic human problems of life as she seeks to unveil truth and teach value. Profound thinking is indispensable because her search for meaning and purpose necessarily involves addressing deep, long-term issues.

The blessed ambiguity of language is intrinsic in this quest. Words and narrative are needed to express the mystery and facilitate the creativity of the divine-human relationship. As we noted above, to replace words with images would have been regarded traditionally as a form of idolatry. An image is a graven image in so far as it claims to represent God better than speech.

In the environment created by the speed, fluidity, newness, and abundance of electronic media, theological conversation seems dull, ancient liturgies boring, and the Bible wordy. The authority necessary for evaluation and prioritizing is depreciated and disregarded. The Bible becomes one book among many, valued only if it offers more help than others.

---

26. Tappert, ed., *The Book of Concord*, 348–49.

All of this influences how the community hears the message. Members find the exegesis of ancient texts extremely difficult and usually useless. They read the Scriptures and listen to sermons searching for tidbits and slogans that might help them cope with their personal problems. Words like "faith," "hope," and "love" are taken from the narrative of creation's redemption and placed in the personal journey of each individual. The preacher is not expected to proclaim an accredited message from God but rather to help each person navigate the passages of their life. The scholar is supposed to construct theologies in the same way Apple builds computers and General Motors assembles cars, designing them to please their readers.

Conclusion

The primary Christian task is to proclaim the gospel in a way that addresses the needs of every time and place. That has always involved using language to make connections with other people, the real world, and God. The question in the electronic age is how to do that with a language that has been enfeebled.

Two prominent reactions believe that this is accomplished by returning to former historical periods. The Pentecostal movement attempts to restore the oral stage with enthusiastic but unchecked tongue-speaking and words of knowledge. Unfortunately, it does this by disregarding 2,000 years of a tradition that calls for canon, creed, clergy, ceremony, custom, and community to discern authentic religious experience.

Fundamentalism does provide criteria but reduces these to the biblical text alone. The first of its five fundamentals, the inspiration and inerrancy of Scripture, makes the canon absolute unchanging truth. The other four—Christ's deity, Jesus' virgin birth, the substitutionary theory of atonement, and Jesus' bodily resurrection and second coming—establish the one and only way to read the many competing and complementary biblical narratives. By placing all authority on the written text, this movement imposes a first-century worldview on all disciplines in all subsequent historical periods.

Neither of these reactions fulfills the church's call to provide a reasonable narrative for the present society. Both either abandon the role entirely by retreating into isolated communities that claim to live by their own version of the story or try to force their renditions on a society on which it does not fit. It is true that the church's history of salvation, which we have been describing as an ongoing conversation, had been the narrative by which Western civilization knew itself for many centuries. It supplied the setting, plot, crisis, and conclusion that gave events meaning and purpose. But it is also true that this privileged position is long gone in the global society created in the electronic stage.[27]

A more accountable response would be to explore how Christianity can appropriately proclaim the gospel in this new age. That would entail examining in some detail how modern technology has changed our use of language and then using these insights to speak and write more creatively. This approach would not leave the field by default to *technique*. Instead, it would add its voice to society's conversation, offering a realistic narrative that acknowledges real-life connections, establishes some norms for creative actions, and provides a critique of the artificial systems created by *technique*.

That is exactly what we hope to do by examining the meaning and interaction of the classic theological virtues of faith, hope, and love. Christians have always used these three to describe how their voices operate in the ongoing communal conversation between God and humanity. A proper understanding of how they function in our time and place enables Christians to know who they are, from where they have come, where they are headed, and what they are to do.

---

27. Jenson's "How the World Lost its Story" provides an insightful analysis of this change.

4

Interaction

THE PROFESSOR HAS NOTICED a significant change in the nature of student interaction over the past fifteen years. Students used to converse with their neighbors before class, after class, and, unfortunately, during class. Now they hardly talk at all. At the end of class, most students pull out their cell phones to type messages to friends who might be hundreds if not thousands of miles away. Very few ever interact with those about them. They are connected to people across the country but no longer to the people in the same room. Of course, they might not be communicating with a person at all. They could just be checking a website or playing a video game.

The professor also notes that student interaction has become much more complicated. Traveling with a group of students back from an experiential learning activity, he noticed two people, a young man and a young woman, planning their night out. While making these arrangements face-to-face, both were also on their cell phones, carrying on three other conversations. The guy was coordinating with his friends about where to go. The gal was talking to a garage owner about fixing her car. At the same time, she was using call waiting to speak with her mother about paying the mechanic. In all, four conversations were going on simultaneously, making this a rather scary exercise in multitasking.

This is even more mind-blowing when you remember that some of the conversation probably involved speaking with a machine. Chances are that an automated answering service at the garage received and transferred the young woman's call to a phone tree, which offered to schedule her appointment or put her in contact with a live person. As she waited, she very well might have been placed on hold, perhaps deliberately, as a recorded message encouraged her to trade in her present car for a brand new one. Indeed, a computer might have searched her data file so that the pitch could be aimed directly to her needs.

If our student had used the Internet to do her scheduling, as businesses encourage us to do, she would have spent the entire time communicating with a machine. While online, she would have been even more likely to be subjected to advertisements aimed directly at her. If she had shopped for shoes in the previous week, she would likely find pop-up ads for the kind of shoe that she had viewed. What began as a person seeking information and making arrangements could swiftly become a chance for a business to make a sophisticated sales pitch.

The students would probably argue that the technology was allowing them to use their time more efficiently. Those texting after class could keep in contact with friends separated by place and perhaps even time, since a text can be answered whenever the other party gets around to it. The couple in the van could coordinate a number of pressing, highly important activities—the night's entertainment and fixing a broken car.

Electronic devices obviously enable new and innovative ways for persons to communicate. The two incidents we mentioned above involved at least six different possibilities: people speaking face-to-face, people using a phone to speak to or text one another, people using a phone or email to communicate with a machine, and people using a machine to hold another in waiting as they spoke with a third person. Of course, there are numerous other options available. Anyone with access to a computer can use the Internet to send messages using Facebook, or even to communicate visually through Skype and FaceTime. One person can transmit their thoughts and feelings to millions using Twitter. Several people can engage in conversation via conference calls. New opportunities to speak with electronic devices are regularly being introduced.

However, even after acknowledging and appreciating the benefits derived from having such an array of possibilities, it is worth asking how all of these new forms of communication affect human relationships. Does the increase in quantity improve or diminish quality? Will using the new electronic devices strength or weaken communication between people? Do they connect or disconnect people from each other, the environment, their past, and their future?

Interaction

Interaction of Faith, Hope, and Love

Answering these questions is important for human culture, but also for Christianity. In the last chapter, we pictured God as a great speaker who communicates with humanity through words, claiming that the divine-human relationship is best described as an ever-changing, ongoing conversation. We also examined how believers understand and explain their relationship with God through narrative, tracing how changes in modes of communication have affected the church's proclamation of her gospel message. Understanding and using appropriately the different forms of communication is obviously terribly critical for proclaiming the gospel message.

In this chapter, we shall examine more closely how the interaction of faith, hope, and love have been used to express the meaning and purpose of this divine-human conversation. Since the very beginning, Christians have used the three words both singularly and as a formula to understand and comprehend their relationship with God. As a result, these theological virtues have become the basic elements of Christian decision-making. Faith and hope inform and inspire love.

This interaction between faith, hope, and love is so intense that it is hard to regard them as separate virtues. The Apostle Paul, who seemed to be the first to use the formula for describing the Christian life, saw the relationship to be so dynamic and fluid that he used many variations of their interaction. He wrote that faith and love spring from hope in Colossians 1:4–6; that faith and love produce good works and hope gives endurance in 1 Thessalonians 1:2–4; that the only thing that counts is faith active in love in Galatians 5:5–6 and Romans 5:1–5; and then pictured all three as defensive weapons in 1 Thessalonians 5:7–9.

This led Emil Brunner to observe that each one of the virtues can be regarded as a total expression of Christianity[1] and Pope Emeritus Benedict XVI to contend that faith and hope are interchangeable.[2] It might also be why many treatments, such as Augustine's in *The Enchiridion* and Josef Pieper's in *Faith, Hope, Love* can claim to be writing about the triad but spend almost all of their time and effort examining faith. Along these same lines, Martin Luther's numerous works on faith end up including the attributes of hope and love as well.

---

1. Brunner, *Faith, Hope, and Love.*
2. Benedict XVI, "Spe Salvi."

This dynamism and fluidity is to be expected if faith, hope, and love describe an ongoing conversation. Our concern is whether the new forms of electronic communication facilitate or diminish this kind of relationship. There will be two primary elements to our evaluation. The first will be if the media preserve the interaction that connects the past and future with the present. Christians ideally base their decisions on faith in the story received from the past and hope in the promises it makes about the future inspiring love as an appropriate action in the present.

The second criterion will be whether electronic media preserve the ambiguity of language that Ellul thought was necessary for holding on to reality at its deepest level.[3] The predominant strand of Christian tradition agrees with him that the richest and fullest expression of human as well as divine-human conversation is the word spoken face-to-face, as it maintains the vulnerability essential to unconditional commitment.

Interaction versus Interactivity

We can begin with insights derived from the interdisciplinary studies made by Paul Ferber, Franz Foltz, and Rudy Pugliese.[4] The three examined from the perspective of political science, sociology, and communications how every level of government presently uses computer-mediated technology. Responding to the common perception that interactivity is at the heart of the Internet, agencies presumed that building a webpage was all it would take to enable more citizen involvement in governmental affairs. In order to examine claims that these projects promoted public participation, cyberdemocracy, and transparency, Ferber, Foltz, and Pugliese tried to define what is involved in interactivity.

Communicating with a Machine

Significant for our work, they found that studies prior to the advent of the computer regarded interactivity as a property of the communication process that used face-to-face conversation as the model. Sheizaf Rafaeli defined interactivity as "an expression of the extent that, in a given series of communications exchanges, any third (or later) transmission (or message)

---

3. Ellul, *Living Faith*.
4. Ferber et al., "The Internet and Participation."

is related to the degree to which previous exchanges referred to even earlier transmissions."⁵ In other words, the exchange builds on previous exchanges, modifying the outcome at each step. Louisa Ha and Lincoln James saw synchronous communication, such as back-and-forth conversation, as the key element of this interactivity.⁶ S. H. Haeckel described "the essence of interactivity" as an "exchange."⁷ All of these scholars believed that interactive communication demanded two or more people listening to each other so that they could modify their communications based on the previous input. The standard and ideal for communication was an ongoing conversation between two people.

After the computer hit the scene, all sorts of definitions emerged. Most were based on the properties of the specific medium being used rather than a conversation between people. Interactivity was judged on how the design of the machine was utilized rather than by any external standard. The assumption was obviously that interactivity was taking place simply because technicians had declared it was at the heart of the Internet. Computers by their definition allowed us to interact.

The definitions covered a wide range of possibilities. On one end, interactivity was defined as enabling the user to modify the exchange in any way at all.

> In interactive systems, a customer controls the content of the interaction, requesting or giving information . . . . The hallmark of these new media is their interactivity—the consumer and the manufacturer enter into dialogue in a way not previously possible.⁸

On the other end, interactivity was defined as simply thinking that you are engaging in interaction. Social relativists, such as Kiousis, wrote that interactivity "refers to the ability of users to perceive the experience to be a simulation of interpersonal communication and increase their awareness of telepresence."⁹

As to be expected, others defined interactivity as a combination of all of these, including process, features, and perceptions. For instance, Heeter argued that interactivity was a multidimensional concept based on the

5. Rafaeli, "Interactivity," 111.
6. Ha and James, "Interactivity reexamined," 457–74.
7. Haeckel, "Interactive marketing," 63.
8. Bezjian-Avery et al., "New Media," 23.
9. Kiousis, "Broadening the boundaries of interactivity," 18.

functions of the medium, which include: the complexity of choice available, the effort users must exert, the responsiveness available to the user, the monitoring of information usage, the ease of adding information, and the facilitation of interpersonal communication.[10]

Three of Ferber, Foltz, and Pugliese's responses are relevant for our study. Noting the lack of any external standards and the precariousness of self-examination, they agreed with scholars like McGovern that the association of the Internet with interactivity had been blown way out of proportion. McGovern wrote:

> Interactivity has become an almost sacred tenet of the Internet. Again and again, we are told that interactivity is what makes the Internet really different. However, interactivity on the Internet is often vastly over-hyped . . . . If you turn a page in a magazine or book, that doesn't exactly qualify as interactivity. Yet, if you click a link on the Web, many feel you are participating in an interactive activity.[11]

The scholars also noticed that a large number of the communication studies they examined used terms such as "customer," "consumer," and "manufacturer" throughout their work. Obviously, interactivity was evaluated according to how it facilitated buying and selling. As we have noted previously, modern technology tends to judge everything from an economic perspective.

Ferber, Foltz, and Pugliese also felt that accuracy demanded making clear that computer-mediated interactivity lacks the depth of human-to-human interaction. Suggesting that anyone who has tried to do business with a phone tree understands that talking to a real person on the telephone is fundamentally different than human interactivity with a machine, they carefully used two definitions throughout their work: "interaction" for face-to-face conversation and "interactivity" for those that include computer-based exchanges. We shall utilize this distinction for the rest of our study.

Interactivity is the more inclusive term, as it includes various degrees of human participation. Congressional offices, for instance, utilize many different kinds of interactivity. They use mechanical responders to read emails and craft appropriate automated answers. These answers usually supply email links, survey or comment forms, and search engines where further information can be found. They might also list phone numbers

---

10. Heeter, "Implications of New Interactive Technologies."
11. McGovern, "The Myth of Interactivity on the Internet."

where the user can speak to a real person. However, all of these are forms of interactivity that employ a technology interposing itself between the two people in the conversation. Rather than fostering a creative dialogue, the technology allows the congressperson to express their positions and perhaps win a vote.

This is a good place to make clear that when we speak of the conversation of the society or community we are referring to this interaction between people. Many question if there is really a social conversation taking place in the technological society, claiming all they hear are sound bites on the public systems and short texts on social media. Academic disciplines and corporate departments confine their thoughtful communication to those sharing their specialties. We believe that below and beyond all that there is an ongoing conversation. Just as Ellul defines *technique* as the totality of methods rationally arrived at and having absolute efficiency, so we would describe this conversation as the totality of human interactions that create the beliefs, customs, and arts of any community's culture. The public dialogue taking place in auditoriums, government chambers, and the media only reflects this conversation to some degree. The totality of human interaction runs much deeper in the flow of history.

Machine-Moderated Person-to-Person Communication

It should be noted that Ferber, Foltz, and Pugliese's definition of interaction does not include two persons using an electronic device to speak or text with each other. They think Marshall McLuhan was right when he asserted that a technology always interposes itself between persons speaking with one another.[12]

We might not go so far as insisting that "the medium is the message," but we certainly think the medium places limitations on the message. We have repeatedly observed that electronic communication lacks the vulnerability of face-to-face conversation. It takes away the familiarity that supports the accountability and commitment that go along with responsibility. The anonymity of the electronic might offer people the freedom to say things that they would feel inhibited to express in face-to-face conversation, but it also fosters online comments that are full of abusive language. The ease of connection accommodates dating services, but the ability to hide gender, age, facial expressions, body language, and race also provides favorable

12. McLuhan, *Understanding Media*.

grounds for bullies and child molesters. These features are so commonplace that a popular television show, *Catfish*, revolves around catching people who meet others online by using false identities.

Electronic media also place restrictions on communal interactions. Their designs offer individuals the ability to make transactions over great distances at tremendous speeds. People can easily use their cell phones and computers to plan their schedules, complete their tasks, register their requests, report their experiences, state their positions, and solve their immediate problems. However, they find it much harder to engage in group conversation. Conference phone calls and video gatherings work for handling business affairs far more satisfactorily than sharing family and community relationships. Online social media are useful for keeping in touch, but rich, sensitive relationships demand personal contact.

Especially relevant to our study, the immediacy, individuality, and anonymity of electronic communication does not lend itself to profound thought. It is designed for conveying short messages, not lengthy narratives. Online users can state their positions on controversial topics, such as torture, mass surveillance, invasion of privacy, and drone strikes, but they find it very difficult to discuss them in depth. The bottom line is that the electronic suits the exchange of information but not wisdom. Few people turn to electronic media when asking who they are, from where they come, where they are headed, or what they are to do.

The Loss of Culture

Along with the loss of profound thought goes the ability to deal with cultural issues. It would not be fair or accurate to blame the prevalence of electronic media for the loss of cultural values. Their devitalization has been going on for a long time. However, the growth of the electronic has exacerbated the decline.

In *The World Beyond Your Head: On Becoming an Individual in an Age of Distraction,* Matthew B. Crawford used strong language to speak of the cultural damage done by electronic media. He claimed that technology distracts people from the actual situation by creating an illusion of control with Disney-like images that deny any friction with reality. He called technology the Great Mommy who responds to our every need by providing handy-dandy machines that solve any problem with the push of a button.

"One click" and Amazon delivers whatever you want in a single business day.

Above all, Crawford maintained that the virtual reality of the Internet completes the Enlightenment project that seeks free choice for the autonomous individual. When cyberspace replaces the temporal world with an eternal abstraction, it effectively removes all authority. The result is a "value agnosticism" that disqualifies any inheritance from the past, effectively inhibiting the autonomous individual from extracting common sense from the "stimulus flux" of everyday life.[13]

Crawford claimed that the vacuum left when cultural authority is lost is filled by consumer capitalism, which he saw as another natural development of Enlightenment thinking. The allure of electronic devices diverts attention from how architects of choice use manufactured experiences to manipulate customers.[14] This reflects Ferber, Foltz, and Pugliese's observation that a large number of communication studies instinctively use terms such as "customer," "consumer," and "manufacturer." The limited interactivity of electronic media perfectly serves the needs of the global economy that cannot function in a fragmented world of multiple local traditions. Cultural values become obstacles to expedient transactions. To insist on taking Jewish, Christian, Muslim, Hindu, or Buddhist values into consideration throws a wrench into the efficiency demanded by *technique*. The cardinal virtues of justice, wisdom, courage, and moderation that were associated traditionally with ethical human interaction are superfluous in this environment. So too are the theological virtues of faith, hope, and love that Christians have used to understand and express their way of life. By default, economics has become the all-encompassing way to understand human actions.

With the loss of cultural values, people in the technological society have tended to repeat the mistakes of the past rather than embark in new, promising directions. Without common values, they become solely dependent on power, relying more and more on the military rather than diplomacy. Language itself becomes a weapon that people use to get their way. Rather than utilizing words to create a common good, they use them to demonize, damn, and silence those with whom they disagree. Having lost the skill of conversation, governmental bodies find themselves in constant gridlock. This appears to be a problem that technology has caused

---

13. Crawford, *The World Beyond Your Head*, 41.
14. Crawford, *The World Beyond Your Head*, 210.

but cannot resolve. The interactivity of electronic media offers no way to restore lost cultural values.

Bodily Interaction

Crawford tried to overcome the immediacy and anonymity of the *technique*, which he called the eternal present abstraction of virtual reality, by focusing on the first-person experience. He believed that technology distracts us from acknowledging the obvious, that the world reveals itself through our bodies rather than our minds. At different times, he spoke of his project as ecological thinking, embodied cognition, and extended cognition.

As these titles indicate, he readily acknowledged his debt to cognitive scientists who study the workings of the brain rather than the mind. His thesis was that we can regain our contact with reality by acknowledging our natural bodily connections to the world around us. This is accomplished by paying attention to how our bodies relate to the situations in which we find ourselves. Crawford illustrated this by analyzing first-person experiences, which he claimed structure our lives. His book is filled with analyses of everyday experiences, such as cooking, gardening, motorcycle riding, glass blowing, and playing a musical instrument. The skills necessary for success in these endeavors demand that we block out anything not related to the project at hand. They keep us in contact with nature, place, time, and other people.

He gave a role to language in overcoming *technique*'s cultural agnosticism when he suggested that it offers a way for persons to share their apprehensions of reality with one another. He spoke of this as a triangulation, by which he meant a three-way interaction that takes place between two people working on the same project and the project itself. Crawford illustrated this by spending a lot of time examining how organ makers profit from others in their field.[15] Language enables them to share their wisdom with artisans presently in the same trade, to receive the inheritance of those in the past, and to pass on their insights to those in the future.[16]

Crawford ended his book by intimating that cultural and religious values play significant roles, but defined these rather limitedly. For instance, he mused that having a vision of how his instrument will be used in the distant future hones an organ maker's attention and dedication. He described good

---

15. Crawford, *The World Beyond Your Head*, 240–1.
16. Crawford, *The World Beyond Your Head*, 9, 128, 210.

as the excellence necessary for skilled activity and truth as respect for the best more than your present understanding of the craft. His very last sentence read, "Only beautiful things lead us to the world beyond our heads."[17]

If one of the functions of cultural values is to enable us to make important societal decisions, there is some question if Crawford's concept of language is really adequate to resolve the cultural agnosticism he laments. Small groups of individuals talking to one another about their craft or a vague concept of beauty are not enough in themselves to confront the horrors associated with constant war, nuclear proliferation, and the exploitation of the weak, nor the misery produced by hunger, refugees, and the unjust distribution of wealth. The depth of these problems requires us to get to the roots of basic, long-standing human problems. That means we have to see how they are related to people and events stretching far into the past. So too these weighty problems demand a vision of future beyond the improvement of our crafts. When Crawford's embodied cognition focuses only on our crafts and immediate tasks, it can be used as another distraction from dealing with pressing cultural problems.

The picture of brain activity reported by the cognitive scientists whom Crawford believed supported his work actually indicates the problem. Steven Pinker described that activity as "trichromonizing" the past, future, and present. However, the psychological present he reported is a moment of awareness about three seconds long. His indefinite past is split vaguely into the recent and distant, his indefinite future into the impending and distant.[18] This is far from the interaction connecting the past and future with the present that is necessary for grounding cultural values. Indeed, Pinker himself warned that these are temporal concepts that we invest with emotion and morality for our own purposes.

A similar problem is evident when scholars turn to cognitive scientists to support religious virtues. In 2008, George Vaillant wrote *Spiritual Evolution,* in which he pointed to the recently discovered connectivity between mirror neurons in the brain's limbic area to support his thesis that we are wired for faith, hope, and love. These neurons are the source of the positive emotions that he identified as human empathy. They are the product of our spiritual evolution, having proven beneficial for human survival.[19] No matter how intriguing such thoughts might be, there is no way that the tra-

---

17. Crawford, *The World Beyond Your Head,* 258.
18. Pinker, *The Stuff of Thought,* 430.
19. Vaillant, *Spiritual Evolution,* 3, 16, 36–38, 126–51.

ditional concept of faith, hope, and love can be reduced to positive feelings and fuzzy empathy. In this case there is not loss of historical perspective, but the shallowness of defining Christian actions as emotion.

The Interaction of Words

For many decades, artists have spoken and written of the anxiety, vertigo, dizziness, and hollowness that has followed this loss of cultural and religious values. All the way back in 1935, the word-master T. S. Eliot reflected in "Burnt Norton" that the eternally present of the technological society is unredeemable, because it is unable to free us from the past or disclose opportunities in the future.[20]

Eliot's poetry reflected his belief that the interaction of faith, hope, and love that Christians used to make sense of their relationship with God was also necessary to overcome this cultural agnosticism. Robert Jenson described this interaction as rhyming the past and the future when he wrote "God is never past only but the future of every past and the presence of every future."[21] At other times Jenson spoke of the gospel as rhyming memory and promise.[22] He was not referring to the similar or identical sounds of word endings, but to the sequence or succession of events that give coherence to a story, novel, or drama. The rhyme is what unites the whole, bringing setting, plot, and conclusion together in harmony. Something that has neither rhyme nor reason makes no sense. It has no reason, because it offers only isolated statements that do not logically follow one another. It has no rhyme, because it is a meaningless accumulation of data that has no purposive or intentional movement. In that sense, *technique* makes no sense.

Faith, hope, and love give meaning to a play in which we are the actors. They draw us into its story as any good drama does. Jenson spoke of the triad's function as formative as well as informative.[23] Benedict XVI made the same point using "performative" rather than "formative."[24] Practicing the three virtues does more than instruct us about what is going on,

---

20. Eliot, *The Complete Poems and Plays*, 117.
21. Jenson, *Story and Promise*, 162–63.
22. Jenson, *Story and Promise*, 9, 53.
23. Jenson, *The Knowledge of Things*, 206.
24. Benedict XVI, "Spe Salvi," 1.

it also shapes us. Another way to put it would be that faith, hope, and love describe an inspiring conversation.

This rhyming describes an interaction that takes place in an ongoing conversation over a very long time period. Faith refers to a story that goes back millennia, hope to the fulfillment of promises that might be far off in the future, and love to how these play out in the present. Faith presumes that we cannot truly appreciate what is true, beautiful, and good by simply examining present opinions, hope that any ethical or spiritual project might extend beyond our lifetimes, and love that then makes decisions based on this memory and promise. The three enable us to communicate with generations we shall never meet and to imagine futures we might never experience.

Using the theological virtues to make decisions does not supply unqualified answers to humanity's present questions. It can enable Christians to remember what God has said in the past and promise that he will continue the conversation in the future, but it cannot offer absolute, eternal truths to be applied in the present. This is supposed to be a sufficient grasp of truth for making appropriate loving decisions, because the God who conversed with Abraham, Isaac, and Jacob, who spoke to Moses from the burning bush, who placed words in Isaiah's mouth, who questioned Saul on the road to Damascus, who speaks through Jesus the Word, is still speaking to the community that gathers to proclaim the Word and practice sacraments in our time and place.

Paul expressed this in his beautiful chapter on love as presently seeing through a glass darkly, anticipating that things will become clearer in the future. In Romans 8:24–25, he said much the same thing when he described the present state of the creation as groaning in birth pangs as it awaits its fulfillment. John also referred to this unfolding of truth when he spoke of the hour as "coming and now is."[25]

If faith, hope, and love inform and inspire an ongoing divine-human conversation, the last word has not yet been spoken. Participants are forever building on past statements, sometimes retaining, sometimes forgetting them. They are constantly repenting or rethinking what has been said, always redeeming some parts of the past in order to make possible a creative future. Change is constant.

Rowan Williams, who shares our understanding of Christianity's conversational nature, emphasized that faith, hope, and love are participation

---

25. John 4:23, 5:25.

in a relationship rather than a mission to champion and preserve doctrines. In *Christ on Trial: How the Gospel Unsettles Our Judgement*, he writes:

> What we most need . . . is a certain distance from the underlying attitude which assumes that doctrinal statements are there first and foremost to assert a position which may be accepted or contested, like other positions—rather than being there to place us in a certain kind of relationship to truth, such that we can be changed by it.[26]

He goes on to assert that participating creatively in this kind of ongoing communal conversation demands a certain amount of humility.

> The conversation towards truth . . . may or may not lead to conversion in the sense of one party adopting the viewpoint of the other, and if we only conversed when that was our aim, we should experience nothing but very tense and polarized communication in this world. As I said above, it is not that the outsider is by definition right, nice or superior, but simply that the outsider's very presence puts a question that reminds me that my account of things, my way of making the world all right and manageable, is not only an incomplete enterprise, but may be an enterprise that is keeping out God because it lets in the subtle temptation to treat my perspective as if it were God's.[27]

This kind of humility is a characteristic of face-to-face conversation. It is not a virtue prized by the technological society, nor fostered in electronic media. An apparent Freudian slip or typo in the Kindle edition of Williams's book inadvertently makes this point when the text reads, "Humility is a word with negative overtones for most modems [sic]."

Conclusion

For 2,000 years, Christians have claimed that the interactions of faith, hope, and love make common sense from the messiness of real life by providing the memory and promise necessary for making critical decisions about what we should be doing in the present. The prevalence and effects of electronic media have presented a new kind of challenge in our time.

---

26. Williams, *Christ on Trial*, 39.
27. Williams, *Christ on Trial*, 64–65.

At first the new media simply seem to place some manageable limitations on the way that the theological virtues function. If that is the case, the church should be able to understand and correct the kind of interactivity that takes place on them fairly easily. However, our study found this is far more difficult than it first appears. The very design of the electronic inherently fosters anonymity, immediacy, and individuality, characteristics contrary to those proclaimed by faith, hope, and love. *Technique* inherently works to eliminate all mystery, ambiguity, singularity, grace, and contingency from the messiness of life.

For that reason, we support Douglas John Hall's contention that the three theological virtues speak a countercultural message in the present technological society. Hall warns that placing our trust completely on *technique* denies the authority of Christ's teachings and passion. He thinks if the church is to maintain the mysteries of the faith contained for instance in the rhyme, "Christ has died, Christ is raised, Christ shall come again," she must make her first duty the proclamation of faith, hope, and love as technology's opposites: faith not sight, hope not finality or culmination, and love not power.[28]

The next three chapters will look at each of the three virtues in turn before returning to the interaction of the triad. They will examine how modern technology has changed the way many in the pews hear the words "faith, hope, and love," considering what this means for society in general and Christianity specifically.

---

28. Hall, *The Cross*, 193.

5

Faith

WE SEEM TO MOVE constantly from one crisis to another. Every day the news focuses on another financial collapse, terrorist bombing, or military activity. We hear disturbing reports about security breaches at major businesses, shootings by those who are supposed to protect us, and outbreaks of new diseases. The media tends to provide almost instantaneous coverage but little in-depth explanation. After repeating the same few comments over and over, they inevitably turn to an expert who supposedly understands the situation. However, rather than sharing their knowledge, this authority figure will instead ask us to trust them. After being bombarded by political posturing and speculative opinion, we are asked to simply have confidence in the word of this specialist who claims to know what is going on. There is no need for us to panic because they have everything under control.

In reality, we are being asked to trust the agency for which this person speaks. If polls reveal that the public has lost trust in this original spokesperson, the leadership will just replace them with another supposed expert. Though the face changes, it will still be someone from within the same agency. We are not to worry because this group of experts has the information needed and will make the proper decisions for us.

The situation becomes cloudier when we remember that these people who are asking us to trust them to come up with the solution to the current problem are usually the very ones who got us into the mess in the first place. They are asking us to trust the system on which the agency is built. It is not a matter of making decisions at all, but of relaxing and letting the system correct itself. Often we are reassured with later findings that the crisis was caused by human error, as if this suggests that we have no reason to become cynical, fatalistic, or indifferent in light of what has happened. To err is human, but this does not negate the effectiveness of the system that is in place to manage our world.

These typical responses to societal crises are critical in understanding the role of trust in our technological society. First and foremost, they indicate that society still thinks trust is essential for its well-being. No matter how much we talk about the importance of specialized knowledge, we still rely on our trust in experts, agencies, and especially technological systems to keep things working. However, the role played by these entities also indicates a change, a significant change, from the way that our culture previously defined traditional trust and religious faith. As we shall see, this change has led many to speak of a crisis of trust, which we associate with a crisis of faith.

Trust and Faith

Generally, people use the word *trust* in secular contexts and *faith* in religious ones. They speak of trusting people or systems and of having faith in God. For most of our study, we shall use the words interchangeably, as we believe that both words express the same idea. When people say that they have faith in a religious promise or trust in a technological system, they are indicating where they place their confidence or on what they depend.

We feel justified in doing this because, in almost all cases, the biblical words used for faith can be translated as "trust." In Hebrew, Greek, and Latin, trust can also mean either human faith in God or God's faithfulness to humans. This means that we can examine how technology has affected faith by examining not only how it treats religion, but also how it has changed traditional trust in general.

Traditional Trust

Erik Erikson, the highly respected father of developmental psychology, saw traditional trust as the foundation of a healthy personal identity. He referred to this basic trust as a virtue learned in the first year of life, when we experience the repeated absence and return of our mothers. All the later stages of development depend on acquiring this basic trust rather than fear.¹ It provides the feelings of coherence, continuity, and dependability that enable us to relate appropriately to other persons and our environment.

Jane Mansbridge and Sissela Bok examine this basic trust in a social context, believing that it is necessary for organized communities to function. Mansbridge writes:

> A modicum of trust greases the wheels of commerce, politics, and social life. Large-scale economies and polities must generate this modicum of trust among strangers. Stranger-to-stranger transactions are most efficient if they can draw on reliable sources of situation-specific and more generalized trust, secured by social and institutional sanctions that punish breaches of trust and by a moral basis for trustworthiness in individual consciences. All this is well known.²

Bok thinks this kind of trust is implicitly linked with promise. When we trust someone, we have confidence that they will keep their word. She writes:

> The function of the principle of veracity is evident when we think of trust: that you will treat me fairly, that you will have my interests at heart, that you will do me no harm. But if I do not trust your word, can I have genuine trust in the first three? If there is no confidence in the truthfulness of others, is there any way to assess their fairness, their intention to help or to harm? How, then, can they be trusted? Whatever matters to human beings, trust is the atmosphere in which it happens.³

She continues that "trust in some degree of veracity functions as a foundation of relations among human beings: when this trust shatters or wears away, institutions collapse."⁴ Thus, trust is the very foundation of society. Without it we would return to a world of anarchy. "[T]rust is a social good to be protected just as much as the air we breathe or the water we drink. When it is damaged, the community as a whole suffers; and when it is destroyed, societies falter and collapse."⁵

While affirming the basic role it plays in any society, most scholars also acknowledge the inherent tenuousness of traditional trust. No matter

---

1. Erikson, *Identity*, 82.
2. Mansbridge, "Altruistic Trust," 291.
3. Bok, *Lying*, 31.
4. Bok, *Lying*, 31.
5. Bok, *Lying*, 26–27.

how much we try to make a transaction more secure by adding a legal agreement, monetary collateral, or penalty provision, one easily breaks a promise with the simple decision to no longer honor it. As a medieval riddle noted, a promise is so fragile that a child can break it and so strong that it holds a nation together.

Religious Faith

Erikson believed that religion plays an essential role in the development of a full human life and, consequently, in the functioning of trust in society. Its rituals celebrate a faith in God and other people that reinforces the basic trust learned in our early childhood experiences. In fact, Erikson thought that if religion lost its authority, society would find something to fulfill the role of the sacred.[6] Many of the scholars we cite in the rest of this chapter think *technique* has provided that replacement.

The classic understanding of faith is Jesus' teaching in the Sermon on the Mount that Matthew used to summarize his teachings.

> Therefore I tell you, do not be anxious about your life, what you will eat or what you will drink, or about your body, what you will wear. Is not life more than food, and the body more than clothing? Look at the birds of the air; they neither sow nor reap nor gather into barns, and yet your heavenly Father feeds them. Are you not of more value than they? And can any of you by worrying add a single hour to your span of life? And why do you worry about clothing? Consider the lilies of the field, how they grow; they neither toil nor spin, yet I tell you, even Solomon in all his glory was not clothed like one of these. But if God so clothes the grass of the field, which is alive today and tomorrow is thrown into the oven, will he not much more clothe you—you of little faith? Therefore do not worry, saying, "What will we eat?" or "What will we drink?" or "What will we wear?" For it is the Gentiles who strive for all these things; and indeed your heavenly Father knows that you need all these things. But strive first for the kingdom of God and his righteousness, and all these things will be given to you as well. So do not worry about tomorrow, for tomorrow will bring worries of its own. Today's trouble is enough for today.[7]

---

6. Erickson, *Identity*, 106.
7. Matthew 6:25–34.

The ability to cope with the anxiety of life's constant uncertainties begins with faith that God cares for even the most insignificant and fragile in his creation. God is in control and cognizant of our needs before we can even express them. Earlier in the sermon, Jesus referred to God providing sun and rain for both good and evil people, implying that faith recognizes a benevolent property in creation.

Martin Luther based his entire theology on faith. Anyone who has studied this leader of the Protestant Reformation knows that he based salvation on "grace through faith alone." His most famous description of this doctrine is found in his "Explanation to the First Commandment" in *The Large Catechism*, where he interchanges "faith" and "trust" constantly.

> A god is that to which we look for all good and in which we find refuge in every time of need. To have a god is nothing else than to trust and believe him with our whole heart. As I have often said the trust and faith of the heart alone make both God and an idol. If your faith and trust are right, then your God is the true God. On the other hand, if your trust is false and wrong, then you have not the true God. For these two belong together, faith and God. That to which your heart clings and entrusts itself is, I say, really your God.[8]

Contrary to the popular opinion that Luther spoke of faith being a passport into heaven, he obviously regarded it as the trust necessary for living according to God's will here and now. He simply claimed that the source of this trust was a divine rather than a human promise. Your god is that on which you ultimately depend to provide, protect, and preserve everything you need.

> We are to trust God alone, and turn to him, expecting from him only good things; for it is he who gives us body, life, food, drink, nourishment, health, protection, peace, and all temporal and eternal blessings. It is he who protects us from evil, he who saves and delivers us when any evil befalls. It is God alone, I have often enough repeated, from whom we receive all that is good and by whom we are delivered from all evil . . . . Athough much that is good comes to us from men we receive it all from God through his command and ordinance. Our parents and all authorities—in short, all people placed in the position of neighbors—have received the command to do us all kinds of good. So we receive our blessings not from them, but from God through them. Creatures

---

8. Tappert, ed., *The Book of Concord*, 365.

are only the hands, channels, and means through which God bestows all blessings. For example, he gives to the mother breasts and milk for her infant, and he gives grain and all kinds of fruits from the earth for man's nourishment—things that no creature could produce by himself.[9]

Obviously, Luther believed that the source of this basic trust is the Father of Jesus Christ. To have faith in God is not to believe that there is a god, but rather to trust that a particular god can deliver on his promises. It is not primarily belief in doctrines or teachings about this particular god, but faith that God loves and cares for us.

In more recent history, H. Richard Niebuhr associated traditional trust with religious faith. He observed that trust, or distrust, is a part of all of our encounters with other people. Whenever we enter into the most important human relationships, those that form us, those that make us who we are, we enter with a promise.[10] He described faith in virtually the same way as "the mode of self-existence which comes to appearance in the making, keeping, and breaking of promises." Undergirding this identification is Niebuhr's understanding that all human relationships are ultimately covenantal. Just as humans seek cooperation by binding themselves to other humans with promises, so God and humans bind themselves to one another in the same way.[11]

The Crisis in Trust and Faith

There is a general perception that we are presently experiencing a crisis of both trust and faith. Our acquaintances regularly claim, "You can't trust anyone anymore." Scholars point to a number of empirical studies that seem to back this up. The World Values Survey, which has taken sample surveys of about 70 percent of the world's population since 1981, probably publishes the most prestigious of these studies. Its network of social scientists bases its findings on answers given to vague questions such as "Generally speaking, would you say that most people can be trusted?" or "Would you say you can't be too careful in dealing with people?" These studies indicate that the number of people who say that they trust others has steadily declined over recent decades. In 1960, about 55 percent of

---

9. Tappert, ed., *The Book of Concord*, 367–68.
10. Niebuhr, *The Responsible Self*, 118.
11. Niebuhr, *Radical Monotheism*, 48, 63.

the US population said that they trusted people. In 2000, only 35 percent shared that sentiment.[12]

At the same time, there is an evident loss of religious faith. Churchgoers lament that worship attendance has declined. The Pew Research Institute's very extensive 2014 Religious Landscape Study indicates that from 2007 to 2014 there was a drastic drop in those who describe themselves as "religiously affiliated." "Nones," a category of those who self-identify as atheists, agnostics, or "nothing in particular," rose from 16 percent to 23 percent of the US population, from 36.6 to 55.8 million. This breaks down into 7 percent of the population considering themselves atheists or agnostics, 9 percent identifying as nothing in particular and not interested in religion, and 7 percent claiming nothing in particular but regarding religion as an important part of their lives.

Although the percentage of younger people who do not associate themselves with a religious body is the largest, even older Americans are leaving religious institutions. Thirty-six percent of people born between 1990 and 1996 are unaffiliated, which is not quite so surprising, but a full 17 percent of people born between 1946 and 1964 also report having no membership in a religious community. Overall, for every one person who became a member of a religious group after growing up with no affiliation, four left. Pew found that the change was not limited to any particular demographic. Significant numbers of individuals of every income, education, race, and geographic area were becoming "Nones."[13]

Addressing the Crisis in Trust

This perceived crisis has prompted numerous studies. Among them, two prominent groups address technology's role, though they read the data quite differently and go off in opposite directions. The social capital school sees cause for alarm if society cannot regain some form of traditional trust. The rational choice school believes that society has simply moved on to a new stage in which trust is no longer essential.

---

12. Hooghe and Stolle, "Introduction," 6.
13. Pew, "U.S. Public Becoming Less Religious."

The Social Capital School

The studies done by the social capital school often begin with a statement about how traditional trust is fundamental in social relationships because it is essential for cooperative behavior. This is usually followed by some observation about how trust is breaking down in recent years, often including the decline of religious faith in its analysis.

For instance, Francis Fukuyama in *Trust: Social Virtues and Prosperity* writes:

> Trust is the expectation that arises within a community of regular, honest, and co-operative behavior, based on commonly shared norms on the part of other members of that community. Those norms can be about deep "value" questions like the nature of God or justice, but they can also encompass secular norms like professional standards and codes of behavior.
>
> Social capital is a capability that arises from the prevalence of trust in a society or in certain parts of it.... Social capital differs from other forms of human capital insofar as it is usually created and transmitted through cultural mechanisms like religion, tradition, or historical habit.... [W]hile contract and self-interest are important sources of association, the most effective organizations are based on communities of shared ethical values. These communities do not require extensive contract and legal regulation of the relations, because prior moral consensus gives members of the group a basis for mutual trust.... Acquisition of social capital, by contrast, requires habituation to the moral norms of a community and, in its context, the acquisition of virtues like loyalty, honesty, and dependability. The group, moreover has to adopt common norms as a whole before trust can be generalized among its members. In other words, social capital cannot be acquired simply by individuals acting on their own. It is based on the prevalence of social rather than individual virtues.[14]

Fukuyama believed that social capital was dependent on shared values and moral norms, common goods and virtues associated with traditional society and religion. He believed that the loss of basic trust had far-reaching social effects, as the school's studies appear to demonstrate that high-trust societies are also prosperous ones.

Others in the school, such as Jane Mansbridge, sought to sharpen the definition. She called it "altruistic trust," defining it as trusting others

14. Fukuyama, *Trust*, 26–27.

"more than is warranted by available evidence, as a gift, for good of both the other and community."[15] Trust is a leap of faith that gives the other person the benefit of the doubt. It is more optimistic than realism warrants. Mansbridge claimed that this enables people to work for the common good rather than simply pursuing self-interest. Responding to many studies, such as the World Values Survey, which report that people with more education and higher incomes trust others to a significantly greater degree than those with less education and lower incomes, she gave religious teachings just as much influence as material well-being. If you grow up learning to love your neighbor as you love yourself, you are more likely to trust strangers.

Eric Uslaner preferred to talk of moralistic trust, which rests on "an optimistic view of the world and one's ability to control it." It presumes a moral commandment to treat even people we do not know as if they were trustworthy. He went on to claim, "Trust matters for the type of civic activities that tap this sentiment of reaching out to others who are different from ourselves—and to helping them. Where faith in others matters most is in volunteering and giving to charity."[16] Uslaner thought moralistic trust that operated without expectations of reciprocity was important in a democratic community, because it fostered tolerance of minorities and caring for the needy.

Social capitalists find it quite natural for speakers to appear on public media asking for trust after a crisis. It is to be expected, if you believe that trust plays an essential role in a healthy society. Ultimately we rely on people, either the person who is speaking or the group that they represent, to make things work.

Scholars such as Robert Putnam blame technology for the current loss of social capital. Putnam's popular analysis in the well-read *Bowling Alone* attributed this loss to the demise of voluntary associations, when television lured people away from public gatherings. Because face-to-face encounters can be very uncomfortable, most welcomed the chance to retreat into their private living rooms, where electronic media delivered pleasure.

At first, Putnam believed that this would be resolved when society inevitably created new kinds of community groups where people could gather to generate familiar relationships. Later he came to feel that simply bringing people together was not enough. Increased contact and interaction can create enmity as well as trust. For instance, meeting with a racist

15. Mansbridge, "Altruistic Trust," 290.
16. Uslaner, "Trust as a Moral Value," 108.

organization can foster distrust. In his later book, *American Grace: How Religion Divides and Unites Us,* Putnam emphasized the important role played by long-term cultural factors in building social capital, particularly those found in the traditional family, religious societies, and government institutions.

The Rational Choice School

It is precisely these cultural factors that we have seen denigrated in the environment created by modern technology. The rational choice school thinks that the social capitalists fail to appreciate the great change that has taken place when they call for a familiarity long gone. In reality, there is little need to trust people any longer. The present society relies on technological systems that are far more reliable.

Some in this group believe that social capital is simply the residue of traditional intellectual and moral values associated with the former Judeo-Christian establishment that are now obsolete and irrelevant. Engineers regard considerations of traditional trust as irrelevant to the proper functioning of a technical system. Indeed, some would say that trust and faith are dangerous. Contemporary militant atheists, such as Richard Dawkins and Sam Harris, describe the religious faith that united people in traditional communities as a divisive force, fermenting conflict in a global society. Cartoonists enjoy acclaim when they draw a picture of the Twin Towers standing with the caption, "Imagine a world without religion."

The rational choice scholars argue that in this new world, modern technology supplies our needs far more efficiently than personal relationships. Ordinary people are not as dependable as machines, devices, techniques, and abstract systems. Humans cannot operate fast enough to keep up when over 85 percent of Wall Street transactions, including the pension plans on which most of us depend, are made by computers. Of course people run the systems and machines, but these are technicians and engineers whose skills pertain to those systems and machines, not to personal relationships. Technology promises to provide what we need, protect us in all circumstances, and preserve what we have: the same functions that Luther associated with God the Father.

In response to this new situation, the rational choice school has redefined trust as a risk management tool. It helps individuals to make some reasonable assessment of who can be trusted based on the evidence available. Much of the school's work seems to focus primarily on how to maintain free market exchange over long distances with unknown actors who are not bodily present.

Russell Hardin, one of its main spokespersons, claimed that what passes as traditional trust is really just familiarity.[17] In the past, people were not anxious about transactions because they were made within a local community in which the parties knew each other well. They could trust one another because they would meet each other in the neighborhood, the church, and the bowling alley. They not only shared everyday activities but also belief systems and customs. All of this changed when modern technology provided a mobility that pretty much decimated local community. All that is left of social capital is nothing more than the residue of a positive attitude, which has no content.

In this environment, Hardin redefined trust as encapsulated interest, meaning that it is based on the expectation that the other's interest is bound up with mine to some extent. It works because the other person wants our relationship to continue. Hardin emphasized that this moves trust from self-interest to common interest, but it does not include altruism or morality. He formulated the trust relationship as "A" trusts "B" for "X." It is very particularized, in that it is restricted to two parties involved in a very specific transaction.[18] Unlike social capitalism, which associates trust with social affiliations and community values, rational choice reduces all to managing the risk of individual negotiations.

The task of rational choice is then to determine how "A" is to judge if "B" is trustworthy in a particular situation. The grounds for this assessment boil down to what can be known about "B" based on the information available about him, and especially on reports of his past performance.[19] Rational choice offers an educated guess on the basis of whatever information can be gathered. This is epitomized by the insurance industry, which makes its bets based on actuary tables and health records.

An even more revealing example comes from eBay. It was originally expected that this e-commerce site could operate on trust alone. This expectation was shattered in only a few weeks, as fraud was rampant. In this case, it was easy to change directions and develop a system based on rational

---

17. Hardin, *Trust and Trustworthiness*.
18. Hardin, *Trust and Trustworthiness*.
19. Sztompka, *Trust*.

choice. The site posted its dealers' reputations based on past performances. Buyers could judge the comparative risk of dealing with unseen sellers.

Rational choice discussions usually acknowledge that even the efficient applications of this kind of trust are extremely limited in our modern world.[20] We have to rely more and more on monitoring and sanctioning to protect ourselves against exploitation and opportunism. We can no longer trust that the passenger next to us on the airplane does not want to blow everybody up, so we require a layer of metal detectors and baggage screenings to ensure we can trust that the aircraft will reach its intended destination. Trust, in this sense, becomes dependent on technological intervention.

Trust and Faith in a Technological Society

Both of these schools acknowledge the major role technology played in the loss of traditional trust and religious faith in the modern world. The social capitalists credit alluring electronic devices such as television for destroying organizations, clubs, and churches that brought people together. It was in the familiarity of these groups that people came to trust one another. Of course, it goes further than that. Before technology provided the mobility by which people could leave their neighborhoods to live wherever they desired or needed, trust was reinforced by lifelong acquaintance.

The rational choice group claims that working towards restoring this kind of trust is a pipe dream. Modern technology has brought a tremendous change that has altered assumptions that were presumed for millennia. The social capitalists should give up their fantasies. Technology has produced an environment in which we now depend upon its systems, not our personal relationships. The goal is to manage rationally the risks involved.

Confidence

Sociologist Niklas Luhmann believed that the situation calls for differentiating between familiarity, trust, and confidence.[21] Familiarity describes the long-standing situation in which people knew well most of those with whom they had contact. He thought this close, everyday contact fostered religious faith in the ultimate benevolence of life and the universe as people

---

20. Hardin, *Trust and Trustworthiness*.
21. Luhmann, "Familiarity, Confidence, Trust."

easily transferred their personal experiences onto the unknown. Familiarity seems to approximate social capital.

He believed that the technological society has introduced risk as a new dimension that must be take into consideration. Present-day decision-making involves the risk of unexpected consequences, resulting not from the hidden ways of nature or the unknown intentions of God but from the far-ranging powerful effects of our own actions. In this context, Luhmann restricted trust to personal decisions that involve risk but offer possibilities warranting the gamble. Actions are based on credence or credentials. We trust others either because our past experience with people indicates that we can presume this or because they come with documentation that gives us reason to believe we can. This seems to be the encapsulated interest used by the rational choice school.

However, Luhmann thought that both familiarity and trust were being steadily replaced in most areas of modern society by confidence in the technological systems that run and control just about everything. He described it this way:

> I want to propose a distinction between confidence and trust. Both concepts refer to expectations which may lapse into disappointments. The normal case is that of confidence. You are confident that your expectations will not be disappointed: that politicians will try to avoid war, that cars will not break down or suddenly leave the street and hit you on your Sunday afternoon walk. You cannot live without forming expectations with respect to contingent events and you have to neglect, more or less, the possibility of disappointment. You neglect this because it is a very rare possibility, but also because you do not know what else to do. The alternative is to live in a state of permanent uncertainty and to withdraw expectations without having anything with which to replace them.[22]

Because personal relationships play an increasingly limited role in the technological society, people see less relevance for traditional trust and religious faith anymore. Decisions are made in the context of technology's power to change things, not in the need for accommodating to religious destiny or cosmological chance. As a result, people find themselves depending on devices, machines, and systems whose workings they do not understand. In order to cope, they leave decisions in the public realm to

---

22. Luhmann, "Familiarity, Confidence, Trust," 96.

specialists who comprehend how these things work, or who at least claim to understand.

Luhmann asserted that people rely on these systems because they have no other choice. They "do not know what else to do." Although technology enables them to control more and more of their private lives, public policy decisions are made for them. Confidence simply assumes that the systems will function as they want and that specialists are capable of handling their responsibilities.

At the end of this sociological analysis, Luhmann expressed his personal concern about people's ability to make important societal decisions in the future. He warns that people will increasingly need to consider the damaging consequences of their own actions or omissions.

> If this is true our rationalities will, as a matter of course, require risk-taking; and risk-taking will as far as others are involved, require trust. And again, if this is true, we are likely to enter sooner or later into the vicious circle of not risking trust, losing possibilities of rational action, losing confidence in the system, and so on being that much less prepared to risk trust at all. We may then continue to live with a new type of anxiety about the future outcome of present decisions, and with a general suspicion of dishonest dealings.[23]

Many of us believe that little more than fifteen years after he wrote these words, fear has replaced anxiety. People have lost confidence in the systems on which they once depended. Although feeling helpless to make significant changes, they have moved rapidly from anxiety about future uncertainty to worry about present dangers.

Technological Fragility

Langdon Winner claimed that a good deal of this worry is warranted on examining the vulnerability of technological systems.[24] Their designs assume that no one will disrupt their functioning. However, he warned that most of our infrastructure, such as the electric grid or gas pipelines, is easily susceptible to terrorist attacks, human error, and mechanical breakdown.

His concern is echoed in a study done by the Defense Advanced Research Projects Agency and the National Security Agency, which

23. Luhmann, "Familiarity, Confidence, Trust," 105.
24. Winner, "Complexity, Trust, and Terror."

acknowledges, "[e]xperts have known for some time that networked information systems are not trustworthy and that the technology to make them trustworthy has not, by and large, been at hand."[25] *Trust in Cyberspace* reports on the committee's work. It begins:

> The nation's security and economy rely on infrastructures of communication, finance, energy distribution, and transportation—all increasingly dependent on networked information systems. When these networked information systems perform badly or do not work at all, they put life, liberty, and property at risk. Interrupting service can threaten lives and property; destroying information or changing it improperly can disrupt the work of governments and corporations; and disclosing secrets can embarrass people or hurt organizations. The widespread interconnection of networked information systems allows outages and disruptions to spread from one system to others; it enables attacks to be waged anonymously and from a safe distance; and it compounds the difficulty of understanding and controlling these systems. With an expanding fraction of users and operators who are technologically unsophisticated, greater numbers can cause or fall victim to problems. Some see this as justification for alarm; others dismiss such fears as alarmist. Most agree that the trends warrant study and better understanding.[26]

The study concludes that there is a gap between what the public needs and expects and what science and technology can provide, citing as primary reasons the complexity and vastness of the system, federal policies regarding cryptography, and the reluctance of industry to pay the price needed for the task. The report's vocabulary implies that an accident is ready to happen sometime in the future.

The responses to two recent crises offer telling examples of the precariousness of confidence in technological systems. After the financial meltdown in 2008, the chairman of the Federal Reserve, Alan Greenspan, confessed that the popular economic narrative failed. He had naively trusted the self-regulation of the market right up to the bursting of the bubble. When it did not happen, millions suffered personal losses from which many have not recovered to this day. You would think that his words should have led to a discussion of appropriate regulation of the market to prevent this from happening again. However, the financial community, which includes

25. Schneider, ed., *Trust in Cyberspace*, vii.
26. Schneider, ed., *Trust in Cyberspace*, 1.

the bankers and hedge fund managers who had used modern technology to their own advantage, asked the nation to trust a free economy, promising that the system would correct itself if we did not cripple it with regulations. For the most part that is exactly what we did, perhaps because we did not know what else to do. We trusted those who created the problem to fix it and their solution was to maintain the system.

Our response to the threat of terrorism reflects this same fatalistic reliance on technology. Societies have always had to combat this kind of coercive violent action. However, the situation has drastically changed when a stranger might control a weapon of mass destruction rather than a knife. Modern technology tremendously enhances an individual's use of violence and deception. People are continually dealing with strangers who might be wielding great power in a constantly changing environment.

Rather than reacting with increased human contact, society has turned to technology's power. On the international front, it has reduced diplomacy and increased the military. The general public accepts our political leaders' claims that you do not talk to the enemy. On the national scene, it has fostered a vigilante society that encourages carrying weapons. Many regard the NRA's slogan "The only way to stop a bad man with a gun is a good man with a gun" as a commonplace of *technique*.

A similar analysis can be made of how society is handling political gridlock, environmental threats, constant warfare, increased immigration, nuclear proliferation, global financial collapse, and many other current problems. Calls for simply retaining confidence in our technological systems are increasingly being met with cynicism, fatalism, and indifference.

Disconnection

Luhmann anticipated a breakdown of confidence that he feared would greatly hamper the rational decision-making he associated with trust. He wrote that this "lack of confidence will lead to feelings of alienation, and eventually to retreat into smaller worlds of purely local importance, to new forms of 'ethnogenesis,' to a fashionable longing for an independent if modest living, to fundamentalist attitudes or other forms of retotalizing milieux [sic] and 'life-worlds.'"[27]

Another respected sociologist, Anthony Giddens, found people have tried to cope with the danger they perceive by retreating into "protective

27. Luhmann, "Familiarity, Confidence, Trust," 103–4.

cocoons" that insulate them from the risks and fears of the global system. He described these cocoons as very small intimate groups that people enter in an effort to block out the ever-present threats of society.[28] Believing they have no chance to change the system, they turn to therapy as a means for adjusting to the *status quo* rather than to the promises of religion as inspiration for changing it.[29]

This is the same phenomenon we observed happening in popular Christianity. The power of positive thinking school led by Norman Vincent Peale, Robert Schuller, and Joel Osteen is an attempt at returning to the familiarity enjoyed in the past. It redefines faith as trusting that thinking positively is all it takes to overcome the risks involved in modern decision-making. The only way it can get away with doing this is by abandoning the traditional Christian narrative with all its real-life interactions and presenting its promises as efficient techniques that guarantee success. From Luhmann's point of view, that is forcing a parochial understanding into an artificial self-contained picture of reality. From Giddens's perspective, it is a therapy based on blind faith that serves as a coping device for operating in the dangers of the technological society.

In doing this the positive thinkers unwittingly succumb to *technique*, which insists efficiency is the only standard for completing the project at hand. You cannot get any more efficient than claiming that God himself has revealed the techniques you are teaching. Those teaching the Laws of Creation and the Plan for Salvation are subject to the same critique. They offer techniques for individuals to get what they want. The former preaches techniques for successful living, the latter ones for achieving entrance to a blessed space in another world after death. Both provide supposedly timeless secret knowledge that separates true believers from the rest of society, hardly the grounds for establishing a common societal good. Neither has any relevance for public policy.

In contrast, Giddens believed a new common story is needed to draw people out of their isolation. He felt a flourishing community is dependent on this kind of narrative to provide a foundation for the trust necessary for taking the risks involved in confronting the basic human problems shared by all people.

---

28. Giddens, *The Consequences of Modernity*, 39.
29. Giddens, *The Consequences of Modernity*, 34.

Faith

Christian Faith

Most of the studies we have been examining supposed that the origins of traditional trust and religious faith were found in the familiarity experienced in communities prior to the technological society. People transferred the trustworthiness they pretty much took for granted in the people around them into a concept of a loving God, and from there to the assumption of a benevolent world in general. They made decisions in spite of the uncertainty of the future by relying on the benevolence of God and the world he created. Faced with the dangers that can result from the unexpected consequences of our powerful technology, they now rely on making rational choices or maintaining confidence in our technical systems.

For the most part, these studies regard trust and faith as outmoded virtues, incapable of making most decisions in a technological society. From their perspectives, those using these virtues are reactionaries, desperately forcing parochial understandings into supposedly inclusive worldviews. We have tried to show they are quite right when it comes to much popular religion. This is exactly what those teaching fundamentalism, the Laws of Creation, the Plan for Salvation, and the power of positive thinking are doing.

We have also inferred that to some degree, almost all people who hear the word *trust* on the street or *faith* from the pew reflect the findings of these studies. They associate the words with depleted social capital or extremely limited rational choice. Trust and faith do not come easily in the modern technological society.

However, that does not mean that Christianity cannot provide the kind of common story that Giddens believed is necessary for a healthy community. In the present situation that does not mean Christians should force others to accept their worldview, but they can appreciate that it provides a basis for their voice in the societal conversation.

In order to demonstrate that their faith goes beyond familiarity, rational choice, or confidence, Christians can begin by observing that Erikson presents trust as a natural virtue, learned through human reasoning and reinforced by a worldview that has often been a religion in past history. In contrast, Christians regard faith as a theological virtue inspired through a relationship with God. This relationship is the source that is reinforced by natural experiences and reasoning.

The relationship with God is always shared by a community whose common story informs and inspires faith. This story features God making promises that extend as far back as the creation. Early on in that narrative, God promises to heal a damaged creation by mending the broken connections with nature, time, place, and other people. Humans are invited to join this project that will bring all together in peace and justice. God's participation guarantees success.

Faith then is the foundation of Christian decision-making. Trusting the promises of God found in this story commits believers to address humanity's basic problems. The Gospel of Matthew described this as giving food to the hungry, drink to the thirsty, welcoming strangers, clothing the naked, caring for the sick, and visiting prisoners.[30] Luke pictured it as bringing good news to the poor, proclaiming release to the captives and recovery of sight to the blind, letting the oppressed go free, and declaring the time when all debts and misdeeds are forgiven.[31] And John summarized it succinctly as loving one another as Jesus loved us.[32]

As a virtue, faith is not committed to any specific political or economic project, but rather to values by which all programs are appraised. It is characterized by wisdom more than knowledge, meaning and purpose rather than information and data. The basis of its decision-making is righteousness, not specific timeless doctrines or laws. In some sense, faith makes common sense of all other narratives, not necessarily replacing them but putting them in their proper places.

Faith's relationship and narrative provide the critical distance necessary for critiquing *technique* by offering a perspective from beyond the systems in which we find ourselves. It offers standards for making decisions on how to use technology appropriately, particularly in regard to employing the gifts of technology for confronting humanity's fundamental problems. The story is also prophetic by nature, as it must first identify what needs to be healed. This judgment motivates making the needed changes, but also holds people and communities accountable for making them.

The fourth section of Pope Francis's first encyclical "Lumen Fidei" lays out a definition of faith from this perspective. Based on a draft by Pope Emeritus Benedict, the letter speaks of faith as "a light for our way." Francis began by acknowledging faith's all-inclusive narrative.

> There is an urgent need, then, to see once again that faith is a light, for once the flame of faith dies out, all other lights begin to dim.

30. Matt 25.
31. Luke 4.
32. John 13.

> The light of faith is unique, since it is capable of illuminating every aspect of human existence.[33]

The encyclical quickly acknowledges that faith calls for radical changes in the present situation. We have described this as the need to provide the motivation to overcome the cynicism prompted by technicians' claims that they can solve all problems, the fatalism caused by thinking that there is nothing we can do to change the system, and the downright fear created by the dangers that spawn from modern technology's power. We have also suggested that the changes demand repentance understood as rethinking priorities, because old ethical values cannot adequately provide guidance when dealing with the threatening world created after Hiroshima and the Holocaust or the global crises resulting from climate change and human engineering. Faith must provide the courage needed to address honestly and creatively the tremendous perils we have created.

At this point, Francis made the distinction we maintain is critical for using faith in making decisions in our time. He asserted that faith does not develop simply from shared human experiences, but in words spoken from beyond us. God is included in the conversation. In that context, faith is a gift that overwhelms the believer, better described as inspiration than motivation. The pope continued:

> A light this powerful cannot come from ourselves but from a more primordial source: in a word, it must come from God. Faith is born of an encounter with the living God who calls us and reveals his love, a love which precedes us and upon which we can lean for security and for building our lives.[34]

The pope cites the philosopher Ludwig Wittgenstein, who compared faith with falling in love.[35] That thought is echoed by Henry Sloane Coffin, who spoke of faith as being grasped by the power of love.[36] Along these same lines, Jacques Ellul wrote it is not so much that we have faith as faith has us.[37]

Faith in the steadfast love of God found in their narrative is precisely what inspires Christians to come out of themselves and make decisions

---

33. Francis, "Encyclical Letter Lumen Fidei," 4.
34. Francis, "Encyclical Letter Lumen Fidei," 4.
35. Francis, "Encyclical Letter Lumen Fidei," 27.
36. Coffin, *Credo*.
37. Ellul, *Living Faith*.

affecting the welfare of all people. Later in the encyclical, Francis made that argument:

> The light of love proper to faith can illumine the questions of our own time about truth. But if truth is a truth of love, if it is a truth disclosed in personal encounter with the Other and with others, then it can be set free from its enclosure in individuals and become part of the common good.[38]

Conclusion

Throughout this chapter we have been speaking of faith as the foundation of Christian decision-making. It was apparent we could not do that without constantly referring to hope and love. It is simply impossible to speak of faith without also speaking of hope and love. The interaction between the three theological virtues is essential for the proper working of any one of them. As Pope Francis observed later in his encyclical, faith, hope, and charity are "wonderfully interwoven."[39]

Francis ended his definition of faith by emphasizing the essential interaction of the three virtues.

> Faith, received from God as a supernatural gift, becomes a light for our way, guiding our journey through time. On the one hand, it is a light coming from the past, the light of the foundational memory of the life of Jesus which revealed his perfectly trustworthy love, a love capable of triumphing over death. Yet since Christ has risen and draws us beyond death, faith is also a light coming from the future and opening before us vast horizons which guide us beyond our isolated selves towards the breadth of communion.[40]

Decision-making in the face of an uncertain future has always been risky. Christians, like everyone else, were aware of the dangers of nature and the hostility of enemies long before science gave reason to think the universe was indifferent to human purpose. For millennia they have prayed for deliverance from sin and evil, knowing they were including hateful actions from those they knew well. It is true that powerful modern technology adds

---

38. Francis, "Encyclical Letter Lumen Fidei," 34.
39. Francis, "Encyclical Letter Lumen Fidei," 7.
40. Francis, "Encyclical Letter Lumen Fidei," 4.

a new risk, especially with the unforeseen consequences that might follow our own best intentions.

However, the interaction of faith, hope, and love still provides a healthy basis for making our choices. Operating according to God's will is best ascertained by having faith in the God, whose story is found in our Scriptures, and hope in the promises we hear in that story. The faith and hope found in that story inform and inspire loving actions that can save our society and world. It is in this spirit that we proceed to examine hope.

6

Hope

Most people have heard of Pandora's box. A woman's curiosity leads her to open a jar from which all sorts of evils are let loose into the world. Fewer realize that her story is part of an ancient Greek myth that is often used to explain the effects of technology. In the myth, the titan Prometheus is the creator and benefactor of humankind. One of his gifts involves stealing fire from the gods so that humans can forge tools. Infuriated by this overstepping of human limitations, Zeus unleashes his wrath: he binds Prometheus in iron chains of his own making while an eagle eats his liver. Technological advances have consequences both unexpected and dark.

The retribution goes further when the gods give Pandora, the first woman, to be the wife of Epimetheus, Prometheus's brother. She brings with her the famous jar that she is told not to open under any circumstances. Of course, as we all know, her curiosity gets the best of her and she lets loose the evils that afflict the human world. Pertinent to our present chapter, Pandora closes the lid before hope can emerge.

Down through the ages, scholars have debated what the retention of hope means. If Prometheus's endeavor and Pandora's curiosity epitomize technology, is hope another evil prompting humans to think they can achieve impossible goals and bringing unforeseen consequences that only create more suffering? Is hope the only good gift, the only thing that enables humans to endure all the various evils that were released? Or is hope a vision that inspires actions that will overcome evil and suffering?

Ivan Illich deconstructed the many forms of the myth that have come down to us.[1] He thought that Pandora was originally the giver of good

---

1. Illich, "The Rebirth of Epimethean Man."

gifts. The male-centered Greek society changed the story in order to blame women for the evils that beset their supposedly well-organized civilization. In its original form, Prometheus played the role of foresight and Epimetheus hindsight. A satisfying life balanced the two.

Illich thought the myth contrasted hope and expectation, a distinction on which we shall build. He associated hope with Epimetheus, who relied on the gods, nature, and other humans to bring a satisfying future. Hope places its trust in maintaining harmony in personal and natural relationships. Illich connected expectation with Prometheus, who turned to technology for more self-determination. Expectation centers on human innovation to provide what an individual or group desires for itself.

Illich believed the balance between the two worked well until the Industrial Age, when society felt it could create a world in which all natural limitations were eliminated. People came to believe that impersonal technology was more reliable than personal relationships. Hope gave way to expectation as people constructed an artificial world of their own making.

Illich's distinctions are helpful for examining the visions of the future offered by Christianity and technology. The predominant biblical pictures inspire the kind of hope that Illich associated with the Epimethean man. They promise God will restore the harmonious relationship between humanity, nature, and God. Hope anticipates the surprise typical of all personal and natural relationships. From a theological perspective, it is characterized by grace.

Technology's visions range from the utopian to the dystopian. However, all of its promises are based on the expectation of Illich's Promethean man. Expectation relies on controlled processes and techniques. Its optimism is based on mechanical efficiency rather than the unpredictable nature of human relationships and natural processes. From a theological perspective, expectation is characterized by law.

Christian Visions of the Future

We have asserted that the three theological virtues interact in such a way that the Christian narrative always includes a promise about the future. Any proclamation of the gospel is meant to inspire hope in God's grace because it at least implicitly states what God is going to do. For that matter, most tellings of the gospel story contain this promise in some fashion. Jesus' healing of the blind and lame foretells the day when God will make all whole. His feeding of multitudes foreshadows the time when God will make sure all have enough. Three visions of the future stand out in the Bible.

The Peaceable Kingdom

The first is captured in Isaiah's beautiful picture.

> No more shall there be in it an infant that lives but a few days, or an old person who does not live out a lifetime; for one who dies at a hundred years will be considered a youth, and one who falls short of a hundred will be considered accursed. They shall build houses and inhabit them; they shall plant vineyards and eat their fruit. They shall not build and another inhabit; they shall not plant and another eat; for like the days of a tree shall the days of my people be, and my chosen shall long enjoy the work of their hands. They shall not labor in vain, or bear children for calamity, for they shall be offspring blessed by the Lord—and their descendants as well. Before they call I will answer, while they are yet speaking I will hear.[2]

> The wolf shall live with the lamb, the leopard shall lie down with the kid, the calf and the lion and the fatling together, and a little child shall lead them. The cow and the bear shall graze, their young shall lie down together; and the lion shall eat straw like the ox. The nursing child shall play over the hole of the asp, and the weaned child shall put its hand on the adder's den. They will not hurt or destroy on all my holy mountain; for the earth will be full of the knowledge of the Lord as the waters cover the sea.[3]

This peaceable kingdom vision presents hope in a pastoral setting, promising a restoration of the garden of Eden. Humans, animals, and the land will again live together in harmony. Of course, the prophet is not literally talking about wolves that walk on four legs or snakes that slither on their bellies. His vision pictures a world without warfare or violence of any kind. The safety that peace provides enables people to have all they need.

---

2. Isa 65:20–24.
3. Isa 11:6–10.

Hope

The Just Society

The second vision employs the image of the resurrected Jesus returning to bring justice to the Earth. Christians regard its movement as the mystery of faith, recited at their Eucharist, "Christ has died, Christ is risen, Christ will come again." The intention of the early church was made quite clear when she used the Greek word *parousia,* which is best translated as presence, to describe this second coming. Christ will be present to establish a just society.

Because many visions of the *parousia,* such as Mark 13, employ an ancient apocalyptic language, they are frequently misread as destroying the Earth and with it any meaningful future for our world. Many evangelical theologians describe the victorious Lord returning, but then immediately turning around and heading back to heaven with his chosen people. To be saved is to be snatched from the Earth before it is completely destroyed. Tim LaHaye and Jerry Jenkins in their popular *Left Behind* series add to the horror by depicting the saints watching from heaven as their dear friends and beloved world go up in smoke.

This is a complete corruption of the texts that really describe Jesus returning to bring justice to the earth. Interpretations like LaHaye's rapture turn foundational passages such as 1 Thessalonians 4:16–25 on their heads. A close reading sees that Paul described Jesus returning to Earth with the saints who have died. Before he reaches Earth, the faithful who are still living join the procession that then continues on its way to establish a just society. Paul's intention to describe a healthy society on Earth was quite evident when he dropped the apocalyptic language in Romans 8:18–26 and spoke of the creation groaning with birth pains as God prepares to set it free from its bondage to decay.

A last judgment precedes the healthy future, acknowledging the need for purging immense injustice, just as the peaceable kingdom understands the need to end tremendous violence. Because one popular preacher after another has gained power and made wealth by focusing on the judgment and ignoring the blessing, popular theology has come to read the judgment of the nations as destruction rather than cleansing. In doing so, this interpretation of the text loses the prophetic promise that Jesus' rule brings a healthy society that cares for the poor and respects the meek.

One of this vision's most complete pictures is Revelation 22's flourishing ecological city. The vision begins with a promise of God's presence. "See, the home of God is among mortals. He will dwell with them; they will be his people, and God himself will be with them; he will wipe every tear from their eyes." It then describes the heavenly city descending to earth, and continues:

> And in the spirit he carried me away to a great, high mountain and showed me the holy city Jerusalem coming down out of heaven from God.... Then the angel showed me the river of the water of life, bright as crystal, flowing from the throne of God and of the Lamb through the middle of the street of the city. On either side of the river is the tree of life with its twelve kinds of fruit, producing its fruit each month; and the leaves of the tree are for the healing of the nations. Nothing accursed will be found there anymore. But the throne of God and of the Lamb will be in it, and his servants will worship him; they will see his face, and his name will be on their foreheads. And there will be no more night; they need no light of lamp or sun, for the Lord God will be their light, and they will reign forever and ever. And he said to me, "These words are trustworthy and true, for the Lord, the God of the spirits of the prophets, has sent his angel to show his servants what must soon take place. "See, I am coming soon!"[4]

The just society promises that everyone will have enough. It cares for the poor and respects the meek. Revelation placed the vision in an urban setting where the pollution associated with cities down through the ages is gone. Pure water runs through this city. Its trees provide fruits of the month to nourish its inhabitants and medicine to heal the brokenness of the nations. Previous verses described a city with low walls extending 1,500 miles on each side and gates always wide open. With justice comes safety.

The Beloved Community

The third vision, to which we shall return at the end of the chapter, is the beloved community, epitomized by a marriage feast. This vision pictures God and all his people around a table sharing food, conversation, and everything else they have. It is based on parables such as the Marriage Feast in Matthew 22:1–14, the Great Dinner in Luke 14:15–24, the Ten Bridesmaids in Luke 25:1–13, and the Prodigal Son in Luke 15:11–32, but perhaps even more on Jesus' lifestyle, which found him continually sharing meals with sinners and tax collectors, women and outcasts, friends and enemies.

---

4. Rev 21—22.

The church embraced this vision of a community gathered around a joyous meal from her very beginning. Perhaps because in every one of the risen Christ's appearances he either explicitly or implicitly shares food with his disciples, his community chose a meal as her main act of worship. Every time this eucharistic meal is celebrated, the church not only remembers the Last Supper but also proclaims that this is a "foretaste of the feast to come." Indeed, the traditional liturgy ends with "Come, Lord Jesus" as a plea for his presence in the meal, but also for his return to lead the community in person.

The Three Visions

The biblical visions are dependent on what God promises to do in the future. They are so ultimately reliant on God's grace that Paul declared an appropriate response to be "hope against hope" in Romans 4:18. He made his case by reminding his readers that Abraham, the first to receive the promise, was an aged man and his wife was beyond menopause. If his family was going to bless all the other families of the world, God had to act.

From a Christian viewpoint, all three are renditions of the resurrection. The church tells the story of Jesus' crucifixion and resurrection as a promise that God shall also raise up the rest of his creation in the future. Although the response to the Easter proclamation is often "What must I do to be saved?" the question is asked in terms of "Now that I know what God is up to, what should I be doing?"

The church's answers maintain the ambiguity of real life. Matthew and Mark claimed that no one knows the hour when Christ will return, so all should act as if that moment is imminent.[5] Luke proclaimed that the kingdom is already in our midst, making it possible for believers to live now according to its values.[6] John highlights the paradox when he writes that "the hour is coming and now is."[7] All imply that those who hear the good news of the gospel should live now as much as possible according to the values of the visions.

The visions at least implicitly critique individuals and societies by how they live out the lifestyle described in them. In Matthew 25:32–46, Jesus revealed that persons shall be judged by how they have fed the hungry,

---

5. Matt 24:36. Mark 13:32.
6. Luke 17:21.
7. John 5:25, 4:23–26.

welcomed the strangers, clothed the naked, visited the sick and imprisoned, and in general cared for the least of their brothers and sisters. In Acts 2, Luke pictured the first Christian community following Jesus' call to live as if God's kingdom was already present. Each gave according to their ability and took from the common purse that resulted according to their needs. All were accountable for practicing nonviolence, respecting the weak, and caring for the poor.

It was taken for granted that this demanded the transformation of individual and communal life. All proclamations of the gospel were accompanied by a call for repentance in terms of rethinking what the hearers have been doing. In this context, actions such as sharing wealth or healing the environment are givens based on the biblical visions rather than conclusions derived from human reasoning.

Technological Visions of the Future

Technical decisions involve visions of the future that are considerably different than Christian ones. Like Illich's Promethean man, technicians ground their projects on human aspirations and the systems that have developed from them. They anticipate the best possible outcome of our present intentions and efforts. From the perspective of Christian theology, they are examples of work's righteousness. We shall present two versions of these visions that both presume human progress, but each in a slightly different way.

Technological Expectation

The first is technological expectation, which believes technological progress is inevitable. It presumes an endless growth but generally bypasses discussions about societal goals. The person who best represents technological expectation is Ray Kurzweil, an accomplished inventor who designed print-to-speech readers for the blind as well as other speech synthesizers and speech recognition machines. He has become even more famous as the epitome of the technological futurist since the publication of his book *The Age of Spiritual Machines*. Indeed, he has been granted a somewhat messianic quality among those who see technology as solving all of humanity's problems.

Kurzweil predicts a Singularity that he describes as a point in history when we shall create machines more intelligent than ourselves. Basing his expectations on Moore's law that claims the processing speed of computers doubles every two years, he estimates this Singularity will happen about 2045. In less than thirty years, technology will finally enable us to overcome all the natural limitations of life. The Singularity is the inevitable next step in evolution, a step we by necessity must take. This kind of determinism is evident in the commonplace "If we don't do it, someone else will" that appears in many technological studies. Because we are bound to follow the stream or current of history, the question is not "if" but "when."

Time magazine's coverage of the 2010 summit of Kurzweil's Singularity Institute for Artificial Intelligence indicated what his followers expect.[8] The hottest topic, as to be expected, was machine reasoning. More surprisingly, the close second place subject was life extension or overcoming death. Many at the conference obviously expected technology to replace religion in delivering humanity from death. Some extremists, including Kurzweil himself, work hard to prolong their lives, in order to be around when the Singularity makes immortality available. They take vitamins, exercise, and follow all sorts of the latest health fads.

The third most popular subject, which followed closely behind life extension, was "better sex." This surprisingly appears near or at the top of most futurists' goals. The assumption seems to be that a robot will perform better than a human partner. One of Kurzweil's friends, Martine Rothblatt, supposedly the highest paid female CEO, has developed a robot to replace her partner if she should happen to die. Rothblatt reportedly takes the robot with them on all their travels, so they can perfect its moves.[9]

Technological expectation is concerned with perfect techniques rather than appropriate ends. There is really no need to identify common goals and purposes if science-based technology can provide endless opportunities for every individual to pursue their own versions of happiness. There will be countless options from which to choose. This vision of the future obviously anticipates the day when *technique* will dominate all. Robots will perform in all areas better than humans, even in sexual relationships.

---

8. Grossman, "2045."
9. Miller, "The Trans-Everything CEO."

Technological Optimism

The second version could be entitled technological optimism. It believes progress is probable, but not inevitable. Optimism acknowledges that technology might be used for self-centered and evil purposes, but believes that humans will use it for good if they think their efforts will not be in vain. Technological optimism does address societal questions. However, it thinks the well-being of our society depends not on a morality that inspires human beings to work with one another but rather on the next big technological breakthrough that will raise our standard of living.

The best example of a technological optimist is former president Bill Clinton. In his 2012 essay "The Case for Optimism," Clinton argued that there are reliable grounds for believing technology is bringing better times. He was trying to assure people that recovery was on its way, despite the lingering effects of the 2008 financial meltdown. His essay might be considered an exercise in political speech, as it was part of Barack Obama's second presidential campaign that continually repeated, "Yes we can!" However, Clinton has consistently championed technology being a panacea, often playing the role of a motivational life coach, counseling that the glass is half full rather than half empty.

The ever-optimistic former president made his case for anticipating better times by listing examples of measurable progress in overcoming "inequality, instability, and unsustainability." Significantly, he placed technology at the top of his list, claiming that it offers the means for all people to achieve freedom.

Every one of his arguments began with new technologies providing opportunities to boost local economies. The primary benefit of the cell phone was inciting poor people to save money. Improving health care was desirable, because it enabled people to work. Green energy was good for business. Justice boiled down to tolerance that overcame the conflicts hampering economic development. Even women's rights were equated with economic gain.

> Happily, I see evidence all over the world that women are gaining social and economic power that they never had before. This is good news not only for the individuals themselves but also for entire societies, for it's been proved that women tend to reinvest economic gains back into their families and communities more than men do.[10]

10. Clinton, "The Case for Optimism."

Clinton then went on to claim that improved economies stimulated societies to address basic problems such as climate change and poverty. His argument involved some rather pretentious assumptions. "Forget what you may have heard about a digital divide or worries that the world is splintering into 'info haves' and 'info have-nots.' The fact is, technology fosters equality, and it's often the relatively cheap and mundane devices that do the most good." It can be argued rather convincingly that technology has been used far more effectively in separating the rich from the poor than in bringing the social classes closer together. There is also sparse evidence that the cell phone encourages many poor mothers in Africa and Haiti to bank money for their children's education, his primary example of a cheap mundane device abolishing poverty.

Clinton concluded his essay with a fervent appeal for viewing the future optimistically:

> The Fight for The Future Is Now. Many of the world's greatest challenges today are simply modern manifestations of our oldest demons. The truth is, the future has never had a big enough constituency—those fighting for present gain almost always win out. But we are now called upon to try to create a whole different mind-set. We are in a pitched battle between the present array of resources and attitudes and the future struggling to be born.[11]

His vision of a "future waiting to be born" was obviously built on the old-fashioned belief in human progress rather than God's grace. Clinton acknowledged that these kinds of expectations were thwarted in the past by those who placed personal gain over societal change. However, he claimed that modern technology has changed the game. It can now provide enough wealth for all. The challenge is to convince leaders in government, the private sector, and foundations that we can base economic theory on plenty rather than scarcity. Clinton was confident that if we could do this, they would come together for mutual benefit, combining their skills and resources to keep the market stable, the government functioning, and the economic system rolling. Like many social capitalists, Clinton believed that bringing people together is the essential first step. The second is to convince them that specific projects are doable.

> I firmly believe that progress changes consciousness, and when you change people's consciousness, then their awareness of what is possible changes as well—a virtuous circle. So it's important that

11. Clinton, "The Case for Optimism."

the word gets out, that people realize what's working. That where there's been creative cooperation coupled with a communitarian view of our future, we're seeing real success. That's the reason I try to bring people together every year for the Clinton Global Initiative (CGI).[12]

This kind of economic optimism is clearly a dressed-up version of the old trickle-down theory, which maintains that poverty will be solved by bringing the poor up to speed with the wealthy. It contains a great deal of wishful thinking. Experts from the government, the private sector, and foundations are expected to give up their faith in competition as they explore ways to cooperate for the common good. A situation in which economic decisions are more than ever based on what brings the highest returns to existing wealth must be turned around. A great deal of fundamental change must take place if the next technological advance is to bring more than fresh opportunities for the rich to make more profit.

Technological Perspectives

Both Kurzweil and Clinton believe humans have come of age. Kurzweil's expectation finds no need to identify common goals, purposes, or ends, because computers will provide the means to tackle any problem whatsoever. Every person will have countless opportunities to pursue their own version of happiness. Clinton's optimism believes people will naturally pursue mutually beneficial societal goals when everyone is able to share the vast knowledge already available. He celebrates modern mobility and communication: "Borders have become more like nets than walls, and this means that wealth, ideas, information and talent can move freely around the globe." Both expectation and optimism might better be understood as extensions of the present than visions of the future. Everything is more, more, more, faster, faster, faster, newer, newer, newer.

Both are First World perspectives that assume that technological progress will eventually enable the Third World to enjoy the same affluence and opportunity the First World does. Absent is any notion of a vision informing and inspiring change. Everyone pursues their own self-interest. Nobody is expected to sacrifice or share anything. Once everyone has what they desire, peace and justice will follow naturally.

12. Clinton, "The Case for Optimism."

Popular Theology

Sadly, our study has shown that a great deal of popular theology is characterized by technological expectation and optimism rather than Christian hope. It has eliminated the vision of peace and justice for all by focusing on individual and parochial desires rather than the common good. As a result, it has failed to inspire the kind of unconditional love that Jesus taught and lived.

We have previously used Joel Osteen, the present spokesperson for the power of positive thinking school, as a prime example. He clearly replaces the biblical visions of the future with a technologically inspired formula for success. Even though he might mention all things being possible with God, his dominant message is that you can achieve anything you want if you put your mind to it. This clearly involves supplanting hope in God's future action with the expectation that the human techniques he teaches will provide the breaks and promotions you need for anything you want. One of his fascinating commonplaces, "Expectation gets God's attention," makes the point while even using the terminology we have employed.

Two of our other frequent examples, the Laws of Creation and the Plan for Salvation, pull off the same thing. Rather than offering a vision informing and inspiring a change of heart, both teach techniques supposedly revealed by God that guarantee the fulfillment of your desires in this world and the next. The former presents Jesus' work as teaching tactics guaranteeing success in the present society. The latter lays out steps leading to life after death.

Like technological expectation and optimism, all three of these schools reduce anything that approaches a communal vision to an individual aspiration, thereby losing the transformative impact of hope. When all is reduced to techniques available for individuals to solve their own problems and achieve their own goals, the status quo is left untouched. There is no need for repentance, because there is no acknowledgement of sin or evil. Sermons become light psychologizing and life coaching, offering assurance that God wants to provide you with wealth, health, and a happy family.

Our three examples of popular theology also follow the lead of expectation and optimism in reading the American Dream as economic opportunity. A Baylor University study and an Associated Press-CNBC survey indicated how much this type of economic thinking has infiltrated popular Christian religion.[13] The first reported that nearly three out of four

---

13. Gibson, "'Protestant Ethic.'"

Americans believe God has a plan for their lives, and the second that two out of ten think this plan involves making them millionaires in the next ten years.

Paul Froese, the sociologist who supervised the Baylor study, thought the findings reflected a religious version of American exceptionalism that links capitalism and Christianity.[14] This popular evangelical teaching maintains that God is using the United States to achieve his purposes. God promises a prosperous future if America remains loyal to the dogmas of conservative Christianity and the free market. This promise often centers around a curtain the divine erects to shield the nation. Pat Robertson and the late Jerry Falwell agreed that the 9/11 attack was successful only because, out of anger, God had lifted this protective curtain that the nation had enjoyed for 225 years. They blamed the ACLU, People for the American Way, NOW, and other "Christ-haters" for "throwing God out of the public square, out of the schools."[15]

Christian Hope

This gated community mentality completely ignores the biblical visions of hope that promise peace and justice for all. Dr. Martin Luther King Jr. exposed the banality of this economic opportunity interpretation of the American Dream in his 1963 "I Have a Dream" speech. Delivered from the steps of the Lincoln Memorial on the Washington, DC Mall, his talk has become part of our national heritage. When Dr. King intentionally combined the biblical vision of the beloved community with Abraham Lincoln's picture of the egalitarian society, he offered a perfect example of the interaction of faith, hope, and love. His speech, which was as much sermon as political address, clearly lays out how faith and hope inform and inspire love.

The Story

Dr. King set the stage by appealing to the Emancipation Proclamation as an important step in America's quest for universal freedom.

---

14. Gibson, "'Protestant Ethic.'"
15. Falwell and Robertson, "You Helped This Happen."

> This momentous decree came as a great beacon light of hope to millions of Negro slaves who had been seared in the flames of withering injustice. It came as a joyous daybreak to end the long night of their captivity. But one hundred years later, the Negro still is not free. One hundred years later, the life of the Negro is still sadly crippled by the manacles of segregation and the chains of discrimination. One hundred years later, the Negro lives on a lonely island of poverty in the midst of a vast ocean of material prosperity. One hundred years later, the Negro is still languished in the corners of American society and finds himself an exile in his own land. And so we've come here today to dramatize a shameful condition.[16]

If faith in God involves remembering the story about what he has said and done in the past, it also implies confessing ways we have failed to live up to its teachings. So too invoking the American story entails acknowledging how we have broken its promise.

The Vision

Dr. King then proceeded to elucidate the vision of the American Dream.

> Even though we face the difficulties of today and tomorrow, I still have a dream. It is a dream deeply rooted in the American dream. I have a dream that one day this nation will rise up and live out the true meaning of its creed: "We hold these truths to be self-evident, that all men are created equal." I have a dream that one day on the red hills of Georgia, the sons of former slaves and the sons of former slave owners will be able to sit down together at the table of brotherhood.[17]

Just as the biblical visions serve as inspiration for feeding the hungry, giving drink to the thirsty, clothing the naked, housing the homeless, and caring for the needy, so Dr. King's dream motivates the community to continue striving for equality. Indeed, equality is defined in terms of the beloved community where enemies become friends who share in order that all have enough. After chanting one dream after another, he ends with an openly biblical vision, "I have a dream today! I have a dream that one day every valley shall be exalted, and every hill and mountain shall be made

---

16. King, "I Have a Dream."
17. King, "I Have a Dream."

low, the rough places will be made plain, and the crooked places will be made straight; and the glory of the Lord shall be revealed and all flesh shall see it together."[18]

The Action

After articulating the dream against the background of our nation's cruel racism, Dr. King called for action now.

> We have also come to this hallowed spot to remind America of the fierce urgency of Now . . . Now is the time to make real the promises of democracy. Now is the time to rise from the dark and desolate valley of segregation to the sunlit path of racial justice. Now is the time to lift our nation from the quicksands of racial injustice to the solid rock of brotherhood. Now is the time to make justice a reality for all of God's children.
>
> This is our hope, and this is the faith that I go back to the South with—With this faith, we will be able to hew out of the mountain of despair a stone of hope. With this faith, we will be able to transform the jangling discords of our nation into a beautiful symphony of brotherhood. With this faith, we will be able to work together, to pray together, to struggle together, to go to jail together, to stand up for freedom together, knowing that we will be free one day.
>
> And when this happens, and when we allow freedom to ring, when we let it ring from every village and every hamlet, from every state and every city, we will be able to speed up that day when all of God's children, black men and white men, Jews and Gentiles, Protestants and Catholics, will be able to join hands and sing in the words of the old Negro spiritual:
>
> Free at last! Free at last! Thank God Almighty, we are free at last![19]

Dr. King's vision sang of hope inspiring a fervent love that "speeds up" the coming of the beloved community. He echoed the "fierce urgency of Now" voiced by all the Gospel writers. Many of us presently share that urgency which Dr. King further articulated in the sermon he wrote from the jail in which he found himself for nonviolently resisting the laws of our land.

18. King, "I Have a Dream."
19. King, "I Have a Dream."

My friends, we have followed the so-called practical way for too long a time now, and it has led inexorably to deeper confusion and chaos. Time is cluttered with the wreckage of communities which surrendered to hatred and violence. For the salvation of our nation and the salvation of mankind, we must follow another way .... When Jesus says, "Love your enemies," he is setting forth a profound and ultimately inescapable admonition. Have we not come to such an impasse in the modern world that we must love our enemies—or else? The chain reaction of evil—hate begetting hate, wars producing more wars—must be broken, or we shall be plunged into the dark abyss of annihilation.[20]

The Story of Justice

It is significant for our study that the best remembered part of his sermon is the dream. The fact that it has inspired story and song indicates the motivational power of hope. Its vision of the future still inspires many Americans, divided in so many ways, to join hands and sing together "We Shall Overcome." Chances are if you asked those singing what they want to overcome, it will not be lack of money or lack of knowledge or lack of power, but lack of justice.

Christians understand justice by remembering the Hebrew Passover narrative. As Deuteronomy 6 makes clear, the community is founded on this common story.

> When your children ask you in time to come, "What is the meaning of the decrees and the statutes and the ordinances that the Lord our God has commanded you?" then you shall say to your children, "We were Pharaoh's slaves in Egypt, but the Lord brought us out of Egypt with a mighty hand. The Lord displayed before our eyes great and awesome signs and wonders against Egypt, against Pharaoh and all his household. He brought us out from there in order to bring us in, to give us the land that he promised on oath to our ancestors. Then the Lord commanded us to observe all these statutes, to fear the Lord our God, for our lasting good, so as to keep us alive, as is now the case. If we diligently observe this entire commandment before the Lord our God, as he has commanded us, we will be in the right."[21]

20. King, "I Have a Dream."
21. Deut 6:20–25.

This common story is so central that the Torah commands its telling and a number of its laws cite the narrative.[22] The story binds the people together in a community that recognizes mutual obligations. It informs the Torah law and Jesus' teachings, the morals and manners, ethics and customs, traditions and taboos that give identity to God's people. Biblical justice is primarily communal. To disobey the law is to break the trust of the community.

It is true that justice in this biblical story includes fairness in personal relationships. The Torah teaches "eye for eye, tooth for tooth, hand for hand, foot for foot, burn for burn, wound for wound, stripe for stripe"[23] rather than killing a young man for striking you.[24] At least two witnesses are needed to convict a person accused of crime.[25] Merchants are not to carry two sets of balances.[26] And although the Hebrew is to take special care to protect the weak, he is not to be "partial to a poor man in his suit."[27]

However, biblical justice is predominantly distributive. Even a speedy reading of Torah law finds a special concern for the weak and poor. A majority of its guidelines concern care for the widow and orphan as well as the sojourner or foreigner.[28] Farmers are to leave forgotten sheaves in their fields, to beat olive trees only once, and to take care not to pick their grape vines clean so that the poor might glean.[29] The affluent are to lend money to the poor when asked, without any thoughts about needing to forgive the debt in the seventh year.[30] They are not to ask any interest.[31] Indeed, they are even to return garments given in pledge each evening, so that the poor are not left cold.[32] The employer is to pay his laborers their wages on the day earned, for they depend on the money to feed their families.[33] Men are to

---

22. Exod 21:1–11. Deut 15:1–6.
23. Exod 21:23–25.
24. Gen 5:23–24.
25. Deut 20:15.
26. Deut 25:13.
27. Exod 23:3.
28. Exod 22:21–23. Deut 24:19–22.
29. Deut 25:5.
30. Deut 15:7.
31. Deut 23:19.
32. Exod 22:25.
33. Deut 24:14–15.

marry their brothers' widows so they have a means of support.[34] No one is to mislead a blind person.[35] It is clear that the function of law is primarily to protect the weak and vulnerable. For this reason, prophets warn that society will be judged according to its treatment of the poor.

Already in 1964, Jacques Ellul predicted that without this kind of common story, the technological society would reduce justice to fairness in interpersonal transactions and be forced to enact more and more laws. Some scholars have coined the word "jurdification" to describe this practice that translates justice into law and proliferates laws to cover all conceivable circumstances. Although the goal of jurdification is to resolve fairly disputes between individuals, it has caused the practice of law to become making a deal that is increasingly an economic one. More and more civil cases are handled out of court, not as resolutions between persons in a community but as individuals relating to each other through law. Plea bargaining has become a prevalent practice in criminal cases. There is no need to appear at the bar, facing accusations of breaking trust with the community, if the trial is simply to satisfy criminal abuse of a victim. Many hail these practices as efficient ways to reduce court load and settle disagreements; however they also reduce justice to settling adversarial conflicts that very often resemble sporting events. In this situation, the question becomes whether an action is legal, rather than if it is just.[36]

The Vision of Justice

David Susskind saw no problem with jurdification. In *The Future of the Law: Facing the Challenges of Information Technology,* he envisaged the day when computers will be able to process enough information to guarantee absolutely fair settlements in every legal case. When this happens in the not-that-distant future, average citizens will handle their own legal needs. A few experts will develop packaged checklists available to the public on the Internet. Any remaining lawyers will become more technician than counselor and adviser. Lest this seems fantasy, a quick Google search finds a long list of legal services already pursuing this vision, including Legal Zoom, Rocket Leader, U.S. Law, Legal Shield, and many more.

34. Deut 25:5–10.
35. Deut 27:18.
36. Foltz and Foltz, "Technology, Religion, and Justice."

Susskind's vision of the future operates from the perspective of either the inevitability of expectation or the probability of optimism. It envisages the perfection of the present rule of law, assuming that technology will overcome the inefficient and burdensome ambiguities of justice. Arbitrary and fortuitous human nature will give way to the efficiency and certainty of the machine. The computer's binary process will replace the foibles of judge and jury.

The biblical vision of the just society is a transformation of the present one. Because Dr. King's "symphony of brotherhood" prevails, a multiplicity of laws would be the height of inefficiency. It pictures a healthy state of affairs in which the Principalities, Powers, and Authorities are restored to their proper places and functions.[37] A harmonious relationship is enjoyed between humans, the environment, and God.

The aim of justice is to eliminate conflicts of interests rather than to resolve them fairly. The exploitation and entitlement that oppress the weak are injustices to be overcome. The pollution that corrupts the environment is to be cleansed. Once the vision of the just society has been fulfilled, those of the peaceable kingdom and beloved community are realized as well. If the meek are respected, so too violence is overcome and enemies become friends.

The Action of Justice

The actions motivated by the biblical visions are quite different than the technological. Because the Bible understands justice as a virtue, it focuses on promoting healthy relationships that create the judgment necessary to act appropriately in any situation. Laws for the most part are presented as guidelines or teachings that incite habits of the heart. Actions are placed in a communal context that evaluates them by how they promote peace, justice, and love.

From this perspective to care for a single weak person is part of a long-term mission of caring for all. Overcoming hunger, thirst, homelessness, and poverty is not a project to be completed within a lifetime. Pursuing justice demands being prepared to share one's possessions and even to sacrifice one's well-being.

Those engaged in this ongoing mission must keep contact with reality by facing up to the betrayals of its vision. That means acknowledging that

---

37. 1 Cor 15:20–27.

past failures were not caused primarily by human error and ignorance, but rather by sin and evil. The marvel is being able to hope in the midst of willful sin and persistent evil.

In contrast, technological expectation and optimism ignore those aspects of human nature that Christianity regards as the chief obstacles to solving life's basic problems. There is no need for God to overcome sin and evil if the machine can achieve human goals in spite of them. The action required to satisfy technology's vision of justice is to work diligently to enact laws that cover every conceivable conflict of interest and to develop computers powerful enough to resolve those conflicts fairly.

Hope's Interaction with Faith and Love

It quickly becomes obvious that it is not possible to understand completely hope's vision without appreciating its interaction with faith's story and love's action. You might speak as if the three theological virtues represent different functions, saying that faith gives meaning, hope offers purpose, and love describes action. However, this should not be heard as if each of these virtues provides some kind of specialized knowledge that can be used independently of the others. Hope's vision only contributes to Christian wisdom and decision-making when it is informed by faith's story and consequently inspires love's actions. To deny the role of any one of the virtues in this fluid and dynamic intertwining of the three is to diminish greatly the gospel message.

Our study has shown that technology has increasingly been used as a panacea for all of society's troubles. It has also argued that basing all on technology's potential is to reduce hope to the confidence that individuals will have all that they desire. Visions of the future that inspire the pursuit of peace, justice, and love are irrelevant and even counter-productive to the efficient functioning of technological systems. There is no need to encourage the community to tackle humanity's basic problems if *technique* makes possible what personal relationships could never accomplish.

When popular theology adopts this kind of thinking by reducing hope to self-help techniques, it destroys the interaction of faith, hope, and love. Its teachings are neither based on the promises found in the biblical story nor are they directed to loving actions that promote the beloved community. Its promises simply play on human desires to have good health, fine families, and financial success. Like Kurzweil's expectation of the "not yet" and Clinton's optimism for the "future waiting to be born," these theologies assume the magic of technology about which Richard Stivers writes so convincingly.[38] They use scientific-sounding language to present an artificial world in which confidence in the future is little more than wishful thinking.

W. H. Auden captured the promise of Christian hope when he presented the Christmas story as a vision of the future in his poetic drama "For the Time Being." As the Wise Men pursue the star, they describe for what they are searching. The first says, "To discover how to be truthful now is the reason I follow this star." The second, "To discover how to be living now." And the third, "To discover how to be loving now." Then all three in unison, "At least we know for certain that we are three old sinners, that this journey is much too long, that we want our dinners, and miss our wives, our books, our dogs, but have only the vaguest idea why we are what we are. To discover how to be human now is the reason we follow this star."[39] Christian hope offers visions of what it is to live as truly human people.

Conclusion

We began this chapter considering three questions about hope remaining in Pandora's jar. The first asked if hope is simply another evil whose retention prompts humans to think they can achieve impossible goals. That certainly would seem to be the correct answer from the classical Greek perspective. Hope is utopian, leading to false expectations. The myth reveals the way things are, how human nature inherently refuses to accept natural relationships and consequently brings tragedy onto itself. To base your vision of the future on technological expectation or optimism is then hubris. It is to think humanity can achieve impossible goals whose pursuit brings unforeseen consequences causing even more suffering.

The Christian tradition contains myths that make the same arguments as those featuring Pandora and Prometheus. The first woman, Eve, convinces the first man, Adam, that he can do whatever he wants, even tasting a forbidden apple. And as we know, that sets evil and suffering loose in the world. The Tower of Babel deals explicitly with technology by describing God's anger being aroused when nations try to build a tower into heaven that will enable them to steal divine powers and make a name

---

38. Stivers, *Technology as Magic*.
39. Auden, "For the Time Being," 34–35.

for themselves. His wrath disrupts their ability to speak intelligibly to one another and consequently obstructs the project.

However, the biblical story places these myths in the context of God's determination to restore a harmonious relationship between humanity, creation, and God. God's love overcomes his wrath. He sets out to overcome evil with love, and at Pentecost shares his Spirit so humans can join his mission. Significantly, the primary feature of this holy day is the healing of Babel that can be read as enabling God's people to understand one another's words and thus to have the potential to use technology appropriately.

Christians then should have no trouble answering the second question in the affirmative. In the context of biblical salvation, hope is at least a good gift that enables humans to endure suffering and evil, knowing God promises to bring peace, justice, and love in the future.

The third question—"Is hope a vision that inspires actions that will overcome evil and suffering?"—is more controversial. Some Christians, such as Dr. King, believe hope's visions invite us to participate in building a peaceful, just, and loving community. They speak of our actions playing a role in the redemption of the creation, some going as far as maintaining, "Christ has no arms but our arms." Others believe the coming of the beloved community depends entirely on God's grace. Evil and suffering will characterize society until God acts. Christian acts simply witness or testify to our faith in what God will do in the future. Nonetheless, both positions agree that hope inspires loving actions.

7

Love

A third reason why we should love our enemies is that love is the only force capable of transforming an enemy into a friend. We never get rid of an enemy by meeting hate with hate; we get rid of an enemy by getting rid of enmity. By its very nature, hate destroys and tears down; by its very nature, love creates and builds up. Love transforms with redemptive power.... While abhorring segregation, we shall love the segregationist. This is the only way to create the beloved community.

To our most bitter opponents we say: "We shall match your capacity to inflict suffering by our capacity to endure suffering. We shall meet your physical force with soul force. Do to us what you will, and we shall continue to love you. We cannot in all good conscience obey your unjust laws because noncooperation with evil is as much a moral obligation as is cooperation with good. Throw us in jail and we shall still love you. Bomb our homes and threaten our children, and we shall still love you. Send your hooded perpetrators of violence into our community at the midnight hour and beat us and leave us half dead, and we shall still love you. But be ye assured that we will wear you down by our capacity to suffer. One day we shall win freedom but not only for ourselves. We shall so appeal to your heart and conscience that we shall win you in the process and our victory will be a double victory."[1]

ANY CONTEMPORARY EXAMINATION OF the third theological virtue must take into account Martin Luther King Jr.'s creative understanding of love.

---

1. King, "Loving Your Enemies," 50–51. Written in 1957 while in jail for committing nonviolent civil disobedience during the Montgomery bus boycott.

Dr. King offered an innovative perspective that works in the present situation but is still solidly based on Scripture and tradition.

In doing so he first answers the many theologians who question if the word *love* plays any helpful function when people use it in so many different ways. They contend that it has lost its meaning when people can say that they love not only their God, their mate, and their children, but also their car, their sports team, and their ice cream cone. Love can express moral commitment or sexual desire, personal intimacy or a business transaction, devotion or fondness.

Dr. King responds by describing love as the way to the beloved community, his designation for the just society to which Jesus called his followers. He did this by very carefully defining Christian love as a nonviolent, redemptive agent of change. Love is the transformative force that God uses to make humanity his friends, thereby making it the "only force" by which an individual can make an enemy into a friend or a community can make its foe into its ally. Placed in the context of salvation, Christian love is characterized by a self-denial that is willing to suffer for the common good. Just as God's redemption of his creation hinges on Jesus' crucifixion, so Dr. King assumed that the change desired in the individual and society demands some kind of intentional suffering. Those seeking justice and opportunity for all must be willing to suffer in a creative way in order for everyone to share the benefits of peace.

At the same time, he answers technicians who question the sufficiency of love in the technological society. Many charge that love lacks the efficiency needed to achieve modern goals. His nonviolent approach was battle-tested in the American civil rights movement and proved able to bring about tremendous social change. Obviously, this kind of love is not a vapid feeling for another person or an empty tolerance toward anything whatsoever. Dr. King built his program by teaching and enforcing stringent principles and methods.

New Testament Love

Dr. King's contribution is critical for the church as love is the hallmark of Christianity. Every part of the New Testament recognizes "love" as central to its message in one way or another. In his well-known chapter of 1 Corinthians 13, Paul described love as the essential Christian virtue because it permeates all the others. None of the other gifts, whether tongue-speaking, prophetic powers, knowledge of all things, faith to move mountains, generosity that gives away every possession, or even martyrdom, qualify as Christian unless done in the spirit of love. John gave it top billing by making it the one and only commandment in his Gospel, "I give you a new commandment, that you love one another. Just as I have loved you, you also should love one another. By this everyone will know that you are my disciples."[2] And just in case we did not get it, John's first letter insisted, "God is love."[3]

This is why love has been so all-pervasive in our examination of the way that the three theological virtues function in contemporary society. We found faith to be trust in God's steadfast love and hope to be belief that God's love will endure. In this chapter, we shall look at how love describes the definitive human response to this story and promise.

Although Dr. King offered new insights, his work was solidly based on the New Testament. In the first three Gospels, Jesus proclaimed that the love of a neighbor is intrinsic to the love of God. When a lawyer asked him which was the greatest commandment, he responded with two, love God with all your heart, mind, and soul, and love your neighbor as yourself. To make sure the lawyer got the point, he asserted that these two are really the same commandment.[4] John reinforced this when he claimed that those who say they love God but do not love their neighbors are liars.[5]

From the beginning, Christians, like the lawyer, have had no problem with the *Shema*: "Hear, O Israel: The Lord is our God, the Lord alone. You shall love the Lord your God with all your heart, and with all your soul, and with all your mind."[6] It is the second part, "You shall love your neighbor as yourself," that has given them trouble.[7] People continually ask for a definition of exactly who this neighbor that they must love is. Luke claimed that the lawyer asked in an attempt to justify himself by trying to wrangle Jesus into reducing an existential demand into a regulation that he could manipulate. The evangelist implied that the question was much like Cain's "Am I my brother's keeper?"

---

2. John 13:34–35.
3. 1 John 4:8.
4. Matt 22:37. Mark 12:30–31. Luke 10:27.
5. 1 John 4:20.
6. Deut 6:4–9, 11:13–21. Num 15:37–41.
7. Lev 19:17–18.

Paul's letters acknowledged the need to emphasize love of people by collapsing the two commandments into "love your neighbor as yourself." In Romans 13:8–10, he wrote, "the one who loves another has fulfilled the law." James followed suit when he claimed that the "royal law" was the Golden Rule: "Do unto others as you would have them do to you."[8]

Relative to Martin Luther King Jr.'s presentation, Jesus forced the lawyer to concede that the neighbor is one he sees as an enemy. It is a Samaritan who goes out of his way, exposes himself to danger, and spends his time and money to help a Jew in desperate need. His sacrifice was accented by its contrast with the Jewish priest and elder, who used ritual laws to justify avoiding care for the stricken traveler.

The inherent self-denial became evident when both Matthew[9] and Luke[10] summarized Jesus' teachings by making central the call to love enemies and return good for evil. Paul reinforced this when he defined love as not insisting on your own way[11] and returning good for evil.[12]

The most comprehensible statement about love in the Scriptures, 1 John 4:7–12, clarifies the redemptive, transformative characteristics that lead to the beloved community.

> Beloved, let us love one another, because love is from God; everyone who loves is born of God and knows God. Whoever does not love does not know God, for God is love. God's love was revealed among us in this way: God sent his only Son into the world so that we might live through him. In this is love, not that we loved God but that he loved us and sent his Son to be the atoning sacrifice for our sins. Beloved, since God loved us so much, we also ought to love one another.

It also makes it clear that this is not so much a commandment as an invitation to participate with God in a mission to redeem the world. Even though the evangelist says that Jesus gives a new commandment, it is expressed as an offer, "Love one another as I have loved you."[13]

The Bible characterizes love as caring for others. A special concern of the New Testament is to expand this care from the biological family and

8. Jas 2:8.
9. Matt 5–7.
10. Luke 6.
11. 1 Cor 13.
12. Rom 12.
13. John 13:34.

neighbor to anyone in need. As King discerned, when love is placed in the context of the history of salvation, it becomes a change agent. It is the means by which God heals his broken creation. In that sense, Christian love is ultimately focused on the common good.

Love in a Technological World

The challenge confronting Christianity from *technique* becomes most evident when examining how it affects love. In the effort to attain absolute efficiency in solving all problems, *technique* breaks down loving actions into rational processes that address each aspect of caring separately. Obviously efficiency is one goal desired in all activity. However, there seems to be special peril in destroying some of love's essential features, if you divide it into manageable parts. You might end up with an efficient but artificial system that has lost contact with the real needs of living people.

Specialization

We can begin examining how *technique* has affected the third theological virtue by observing that until modern technology began affecting all areas of life, love was regarded as a relationship in which a person showed compassion for another by caring for their whole person. As the desire for efficiency led to breaking that multifunctional concern into single operations, people began turning to specialists to satisfy their needs. Rather than responding to the needs of the whole person, experts address the particular problems for which they have special skills. People deal with one specialist for business, another for entertainment, another for counseling, and yet another for companionship.

Specialization certainly offers an efficient way to care for people in a global society. It enables addressing the specific needs of someone who lives on the other side of the globe, even though you have no idea of what is going on in their private life. At the same time, this culture justifies passing the next-door neighbor daily without feeling any need to know their personal needs.

Specialization also focuses love on the short-term solution of the immediate problems an individual faces. The expert specializes in problem-solving rather than caring relationships. All that matters is that instant in time. The past and future are ignored. Efficiency demands that only the moment needs to be addressed by the specialist. Love's role as a change agent for bringing the beloved community is, for the most part, lost.

Intimacy

Love also plays a greatly reduced role in the technological society. Although popular songs proclaim "all we need is love, sweet love" and claim "that's what it's all about," love plays a rather insignificant role in public policy.

Technicians regard love as a very limited resource, and so of little use in solving the problems of the larger society. It is confined to fewer and fewer personal relationships because the tools and means of technology are far more effective at addressing peoples' concerns.

Research indicates that fewer people in the present society experience personal relationships in which people respond to each other as whole persons. A 2006 report from the American Sociology Review indicated that people have experienced a significant loss in the quantity and quality of friends since 1985.[14] One-fourth indicated that they had no close confidants. In addition, the number of friends reported by the average American dropped from four to two in those twenty years. Americans have fewer personal relationships, and these are far more volatile than those typically enjoyed in traditional societies.

This leads sociologists, such as Anthony Giddens and Thomas Luhmann, to use the abstract term *intimacy* to describe what used to be regarded as loving relationships. They define intimacy as a pure relationship based on negotiations between a very small number of people, such as a husband and wife, parents and children, two lovers, or a few close friends. These very limited arrangements have replaced the established roles of the extended family and neighbor on which traditional society was based. Intimacy reduces personal relationships to an agreement focusing on what this very small group wants to get out of the association.

Giddens and Luhmann find that intimacy is based primarily on the immediate feelings of those involved. Everything depends on satisfying one another emotionally. Both describe these kinds of relationships as very brittle, fragile, and easily broken. People move in and out of them very easily because their emotional needs change frequently throughout their lives.

Rather than providing meaning for participation in the larger world, intimacy enables escape from its meaninglessness. Its main function is to

---

14. McPherson et al., "Social Isolation in America."

provide a haven from the impersonal rigors and risks of the technological society. In a sense, intimacy is the modern form of romantic love that enables two people to find meaning in their own small world in spite of the senselessness out there in the wider one. All boils down to "You and me, babe." One finds satisfaction by losing oneself in another person, very much as one used to lose oneself in God. Our story replaces God's story, as well-being is defined as being there for this particular other person.[15,16,17]

Social Media Friendship

Facebook friends are a perfect example of negotiated personal relationships. This electronic version of social contact compensates for the reduced number of intimate relationships. However, the terms of the relationship are far from caring for the needs of the whole person.

Facebook friends are restricted to reporting where they are and what they are doing and feeling. One can respond by hitting the "like" button or by making a very brief, and hopefully clever, comment. You are able to express your emotions by using symbols on the keypad, but cannot hug, kiss, or even touch these electronic friends. In fact, you cannot engage in any prolonged or profound conversation using the options available. There is no doubt that you can stay in contact over a long distance. However, this is a very narrow-band connection.

The limitations of expressing love on electronic media come across when televangelists end their programs with "God loves you, and so do I." Their loyal followers might hear this as a genuine statement of affection. However, most others realize that these preachers do not even know their names, much less their needs. To assert love from afar, or when disconnected from face-to-face confrontation, lacks any vulnerability.

This freedom from in-depth involvement is also evident in the ease with which users can pick up more "friends" by accepting the invitations which arrive daily on their emails, often from people they have a hard time identifying. And, of course, they can "unfriend" anyone with the push of a button. In traditional societies, friends, family, and community provided checks on individual self-absorption. It was difficult to drop relationships, because family and friends lived nearby and were in constant contact.

15. Giddens, *Modernity and Self-Identity*, 6.
16. Giddens, *The Transformation of Intimacy*, 39.
17. Luhmann, *Love as Passion*, 174–75.

This is not to disparage the great contributions of the many forms of social media. They enable users to keep in contact with those for whom they care. Even though the electronic offers narrow-band connection, it can augment and support loving relationships made previously face-to-face. Beyond that, many report that they have meaningful and lengthy exchanges involving profound thoughts with friends they know well and within the limitations of the media.

Some find narrow-band connections to be compatible with their hurried lifestyles. They prefer using text messages rather than speaking directly to people on their cell phones because they often do not want to get involved in emotional confrontations. Many situations call for a simple response rather than an extended conversation.

An examination of Facebook friendship leads to another characteristic of love in modern society. Facebook is a business enterprise that forces its users to consent to a long and obtuse agreement granting the company all sorts of rights for financial profit. For instance, it can place advertisements on the users' timelines or sell their personal data to other businesses. Placing love into a technological context reduces it to a commodity with an economic value that can be measured and controlled.

Professional Friendship

This commercializing of some functions of traditional love becomes evident in the prevalence of professional relationships in contemporary society. A recent conversation beautifully illustrates how intimate friendships have been replaced by paid services. A handsome man of about fifty years old sat down next to the older of the authors at a wedding. He reported that he had traveled from Las Vegas in order to be with his best friend, whom he met in the Navy. This longtime friend had stood by him when he had "lost," that was his word, three wives, two fianceés, and two daughters. Through all of this, his friend had offered support and good advice. Sometimes he was the man's only as well as his best friend.

However, they had never lived close to one another since the Navy years. They had lived across the nation and at times even across the world from each other. Obviously, technology provided an environment that enabled the speaker to feel that he maintained a close relationship. Traditionally, of course, friendship was based on a face-to-face intimacy, often over a lifetime in one location.

It was the second part of the conversation that was most revealing. When asked what he did, the man hesitated. "It is hard to explain," he responded. "I work at a famous casino as a friend." He then launched into what was at least a twenty-minute soliloquy explaining his position. He has been in the gambling business for over twenty-five years and has seen many changes. The greatest and most disheartening have been those that technology has brought. Everything is digital now, everything silent. There is no more machine noise, no more jingle of coins, no more sound of hitting the jackpot, and no more cheers at winning. Rather than loudly celebrating victories with those at the next machines, winners are more likely to text a friend across the room or even across the world.

"That's where I come in," he said. "I greet them at the door, talk to them while they play, and especially celebrate with them when they win. I am their friend." He went on to explain that the casino made more money when gamblers stayed longer. His job is to make people feel at home so that they want to stay. "Everything is statistics," he volunteered. "The longer people stay, the greater the house odds. You might not be aware that the success of the casino is more dependent on the little guy than the high roller. My job is to befriend the ordinary gambler." When asked if he couldn't be better described as a friend of the casino, he readily agreed. However, he quickly noted that the gamblers really appreciated his conversation and interest. And he went on to say that most of the time he developed warm feelings for them as well.

The speaker described himself as a professional friend, a role he filled admirably. He was a good looking, well spoken, intelligent man with whom it was natural to feel at ease. The casino obviously appreciated that most people would describe him as friendly and interested in their welfare after even a brief encounter. The irony of the situation is that this professional friend had tremendous trouble with the familiarity and care associated with traditional long-term, multi-faceted, loving relationships.

A "professional friend" would be an oxymoron in traditional society, but is taken for granted in our technological age. Most of the functions performed by a friend in the past have now transitioned into paid, specialized services. People regard their pastors, therapists, doctors, lawyers, and financial advisers as their friends. Caregivers, counselors, and retirement community workers are all paid. Television constantly reminds us that we have a friend at the bank, the insurance office, the stock brokerage, and the car dealership. There are all kinds of professional friends out there.

This is not to say that people are paid to be our friends. If care is broken down into special functions, people must be trained as specialists. Specialists must be trained and that takes money. Soon everything is placed in an economic context and with it worth is measured by monetary values. Love becomes a commodity that can be bought and sold.

Charity

It is easy to see the effect of this commercial trend by tracing the development of charity from the first-century Christian community chest into the present-day nonprofit business. Christian charity began as a love for the neighbor that ensured they would have enough. It was based on the solidarity of the community that saw itself as sharing the love of Christ. Acts 2 tells of the wealthy in the Jerusalem church selling their property and placing the proceeds into a common chest from which people could take according to their needs. Although it is difficult to chart exactly how long this sharing of wealth endured, it appears to have been assumed as a Christian practice in some form for a long time. The apostles created the office of deacon in order to supervise a fair distribution of funds to the needy. Well into the latter part of the second century, the great church father Tertullian, not known for his humor, claimed that Christians had all in common except their women.

Even after the common chest disappeared from her structure, the church based her charitable activity on Matthew 25:31–45, where Christ claimed that the last judgment would be based on sharing food, drink, and clothing, as well as caring for the sick, welcoming strangers, and visiting prisoners. Charity was understood as sharing what one had with others. The sense of solidarity was so strong that Carter Lindberg[18] and Peter Brown[19] believe the needy felt they had a claim on the wealth of the rich in the sense that in the future kingdom of God they would serve as intercessors for the affluent.

Ivan Illich believed he noticed this solidarity breaking down in the twelfth century, when the church began to institutionalize almsgiving.[20] Centralization established uniform standards and guidelines that led to the publishing of official lists of the worthy poor. Efficiency and control as-

18. Lindberg, *Beyond Charity*.
19. Brown, *Through the Eye of a Needle*.
20. Garrigos, "Hospitality Cannot be a Challenge," 119.

sumed as much importance as compassion when generosity was extended exclusively to those who merited it. Lindberg Carter believed that urban governments also began to take responsibility in this period, in order to control the tremendous growth of poverty in the cities. Charity became more secularized, as the churches could not handle the problem on their own.

The next significant development took place in the nineteenth century, when concern for efficient giving became more pronounced. It was regarded as naïve for wealthy individuals to give directly to the poor. Instead philanthropy, commonly associated with Andrew Carnegie, became the means by which the rich could provide opportunity for the poor. Charity was reduced to providing funds for nonprofit businesses directed by trained specialists. Charity might refer to the money given or the benefactors, such as public libraries, museums, universities, and parks.

It was at this time that the social gospel movement called on the government to address the structural causes of poverty. It asserted that a true Good Samaritan realizes that his ministering to an injured person on a dangerous road is a limited *ad hoc* solution. The real, sustaining action involves working for political programs that police the road and prevent such muggings. The strategy for church missions became "It is better to teach a poor man how to fish than to give him a fish."

At the present time only about 10 percent of charity provides basic human needs, such as food, shelter, and clothing, those things associated with traditional almsgiving. Most involve raising funds for nonprofit projects or services, such as symphony orchestras, medical research, art galleries, retirement care, academic institutions, and other special causes that generally are used more extensively by the wealthy than the poor.

Those that do service the poor have become very large businesses and welfare systems operating with cost-effective standards. Executives make six- and even seven-figure salaries. Each part of the operation is broken down into separate functions run by specialists. Professionals do most of the soliciting, as amateur volunteers waste time and money. These professional fundraisers utilize huge data banks, computer-written and generated letters, and other impersonal technologies. Because altruism is regarded as a scarce commodity, they employ techniques, such as public acknowledgements, thank you letters, gifts, donor lists, benefit dinners, and golf tournaments. All of these offer not only "feel good" moments, but also business opportunities.

Lost are the personal relationships with real, needy people. Instead, donors view slick electronic portrayals of suffering that elicit pity and then want to make a speedy financial response, often again using electronic means. Lost too is any kind of accountability except the bottom line on the financial report. Our research found that most of the money given to modern charities went to overhead expenses rather than the needy cause. Modern professional fundraisers justify this by arguing that they produce more money that can be used for good than the methods of traditional societies. One small local charity reported that even though the fundraiser kept over three quarters of what was raised, the charity was better off as they still received many times what they could expect to raise on their own.[21]

The Effect on the Church

The church reflects these same characteristics when it is described as an institution in the technological society operating on a business model, rather than as a community in which people share their lives. It is very common to hear people insist that their church is a business when trying to impress on others that their congregation has to pay its bills. However, this business model goes far beyond meeting the costs of maintaining a large physical plant and a full-time pastor.

Just about every modern ministry has become financial. Very few members personally participate in caring activities, as volunteers are now regarded to be inefficient. If a new need is perceived, members are asked to increase their financial giving so that a specialist can be employed. Most of the caring ministry is now done by professional friends.

Members also participate in caring ministries outside the local congregation thorough financial gifts. They send their money to the larger church that runs retirement communities, hospitals, social agencies, counseling services, and other service organizations. For the most part, these operate just like other big charitable businesses. Sometimes they justify their support by claiming to offer more compassionate service at a lower cost. Often they do deliver more for your buck, because they can augment their professional staff with volunteers around the world. In this sense, they deserve to be considered efficient institutions.

In this model, Christian charity seldom involves sharing self so that all in the community have enough. Most charitable works are limited to

---

21. Foltz and Foltz, "Charity in a Technological Society."

activities like holiday bureaus that collect toys for poor children at Christmas or relief efforts that respond to world emergencies. As much as the intention is to express compassionate love that genuinely attempts to share another's suffering, there is little chance to have significant contact with the needy. The vulnerability associated with caring for a whole person who shares your life is gone.

Too often when Christians speak of finding loving relationships in their churches, they refer to an intimacy that provides security in an ever-changing and seemingly indifferent society. They want their congregations to be havens from society where respectable people teach traditional values. This usually means people like themselves who share their values.

Because most come to get a good feeling about being right with God and other people, a great deal of the ministry is to emotional needs. Sermons are often feel-good messages assuring people that they are right with God. People show up to mark traditional passages of life, such as sharing joy at births and weddings, empathy at illnesses, and grief at deaths. Nevertheless, personal contacts often have less depth than those shared by Facebook friends. People might not even know the names of people with whom they share the communion table.

In this situation, the prophetic ministry disappears as the focus is on adjusting to the status quo. There is little concern for transforming either individuals or the larger society. If their needs are not met, members leave to seek another congregation. If the pastor speaks to a social issue, many members complain that the church should not be political.

Some might question such depictions, pointing to how much churches have engaged in political activity in recent decades. However, most of this is not focused on changing society but rather on defending parochial values. The most evident Christian political action aims to preserve the status quo or return to a supposedly past golden age. Jerry Falwell led the first wave in the 1980s when his Moral Majority endorsed candidates who promised a return to family values. Its program was made up of negative attacks on abortion, women's liberation, gay rights, the sexual revolution, and secularism in the public schools. When it became evident that this group did not represent a majority of the voters, the second wave featured Evangelicals and Roman Catholics joining forces to protect religious liberty. Again, the effort was not to work for the beloved community of the future, but primarily to preserve the right to practice their values in their own communities in the present. Both waves looked to the past rather than the future.

Many church members argue that this is the most efficient way to practice love in our modern society. However, efficiency depends upon the desired goal. If the aim is accumulating a lot of money in order to fund projects that you deem important, then the effectiveness of the present system can be touted. But if you aspire to the beloved community, in which everyone shares themselves in order that all can have enough, there is a question if the claim of efficiency is warranted.

Christian Love

It is important to make clear at this point that it is hardly accurate to describe the church as simply an institution in the technological society. She is also a community that gathers regularly to read lessons from the ancient story. Her leaders try to apply these teachings to the present situation. Hopefully the whole congregation has an opportunity to share their thoughts as well. Many churches express their visions of hope by eating a meal together. In other words, those attending worship regularly are given the chance to understand love in the context of faith's story and hope's promises. They hear words expressing that they are lovable, that they are more than what they do. "God loves you; love one another" is repeated and experienced in a wide variety of ways.

Viewed from this perspective, the church is one of the few remaining communities that has the potential to provide a critique of the technological society. She constantly tells and hears a story that challenges the will to power inherent in *technique*. That story, in which faith provides meaning and hope, offers purpose that inspires her people to make the loving decisions needed to use technology appropriately.

When love is presented in the context of this story, it encompasses the nonviolent and redemptive features proclaimed by Dr. King. Balancing mind and heart, efficiency and compassion, it holds institutions as well as individuals accountable. Three features can be highlighted: Christian love is unconditional. It is best defined as compassion that suffers with and for others. It is redemptive and transformative.

Covenant

The relationship between God and humanity that models Christian love is not a contract, but a covenant whose fulfillment depends on God's participation. Unlike the usual contract, this covenant is not abandoned if one party does not satisfy the requirements. God makes an unconditional promise in Genesis 12. He will bless Abraham's family so they can become a blessing for all other nations.

Jeremiah made it clear that it is God's steadfast love that guarantees this covenant's fulfillment. After recounting the numerous ways that the nation disobeyed God's law, the prophet assured his people that God's promise would still stand: "I will put my law within them, and I will write it on their hearts; and I will be their God, and they shall be my people. No longer shall they teach one another, or say to each other, 'Know the Lord,' for they shall all know me, from the least of them to the greatest."[22]

Paul proclaimed that this promise was fulfilled in Jesus' resurrection, so that "God's love has been poured into our hearts through the Holy Spirit that has been given to us."[23] In other words, Christian love is an infused virtue that ultimately flows from a proper relationship with God.

In his definitive resurrection appearance, John empathized love's unconditional feature. Three times Jesus asked Peter if he loves him. The first two questions used a Greek word *philios*, which indicates a kind of love that offers mutual benefit. The third used *agape*, a Greek word that the New Testament associates with God's steadfast love. The implication that Peter must practice God's unconditional love is obvious when the following verses indicate that he will be martyred.[24]

David Bentley Hart, a Greek Orthodox theologian, thinks a conversation in Dostoevsky's *The Brothers Karamazov* epitomizes unconditional Christian love.[25] Ivan, the intellectual brother, engages Father Zosima, a monk revered as a spiritual guide or *staretz*. When Ivan claims that he is able to love some people and admire some human deeds some of the time, Zosima insists that love cannot be selective. It must be universal and concrete at the same time. In response, Ivan professes that he might be able to love humans in general, but he still hates them in particular. It is precisely the neighbor with "bad breath, foolish face, ill manners" that he cannot love. The *staretz* maintains that Christian love is not love in general but loving the neighbor before us in need.

---

22. Jer 31:31–34.
23. Rom 5.
24. John 22.
25. Hart, *The Doors of the Sea*.

> Do not be afraid of men's sin, love man also in his sin, for this likeness of God's love is the height of love on earth. Love all of God's creation, both the whole of it and every grain of sand. Love every leaf, every ray of God's light. Love animals, love plants, love each thing. If you love each thing, you will perceive the mystery of God in things. Once you have perceived it, you will begin tirelessly to perceive more and more of it every day. And you will come at last to love the whole world with an entire, universal love.[26]

Hart reflects on how this unconditional love is essential for understanding the gospel message. Only by beginning with this virtue can humans find realistic meaning and purpose. However, because they must live in the here and now, they must apply this kind of love to the real challenges and tragedies that they encounter.

> To see the world as it should be seen, and so to see the true glory of God reflected in it, requires the cultivation of charity, of an eye rendered limpid by love. Maximus the Confessor taught that it is only when one has learned to look upon the world with selfless charity that one sees the true inner essence—the logos—of any created thing, and sees how that thing shines with the light of the one divine Logos that gives it being. But what the Christian should see, then, is not simply one reality.... Rather, the Christian should see two realities at once, one world (as it were) within another: one the world as we all know it, in all its beauty and terror, grandeur and dreariness, delight and anguish; and the other the world in its first and ultimate truth, not simply "nature" but "creation": an endless sea of glory, radiant with the beauty of God in every part, innocent of all violence. To see in this way is to rejoice and mourn at once, to regard the world as a mirror of infinite beauty, but as glimpsed through the veil of death. It is to see the creation in chains but beautiful as is the beginning of days.[27]

Sacrifice

Hart reminds us that God's unconditional love is proclaimed in the context of a penultimate situation. Things are not as they will be. In the present, self-denial, sacrifice, and suffering are necessary.

---

26. Dostoyevsky, *The Brothers Karamazov*, 382.
27. Hart, *The Doors of the Sea*, 59–60.

The critical turning point in the first three gospels features Jesus redefining the role of Messiah as necessarily involving suffering. He immediately follows this by revealing that his followers will also have to bear their own crosses. "If any want to become my followers, let them deny themselves and take up their cross and follow me. For those who want to save their life will lose it, and those who lose their life for my sake, and for the sake of the gospel, will save it."[28]

This is not to disparage the self, as often interpreted, but rather to assert that the true self is found in a loving relationship with God and other people. One finds identity, meaning, and purpose in sharing one's life. In the context of the covenant, this might mean suffering for the sake of righteousness rather than using the church's sanctuary as a haven from reality.

Both Paul and John described the cross as the supreme act of God's love that Christians are to imitate. Paul put it this way:

> Let the same mind be in you that was in Christ Jesus, who, though he was in the form of God, did not regard equality with God as something to be exploited, but emptied himself, taking the form of a slave, being born in human likeness. And being found in human form, he humbled himself and became obedient to the point of death—even death on a cross.[29]

John said the same in 1 John 4 when he wrote, "In this is love, not that we loved God but that he loved us and sent his Son to be the atoning sacrifice for our sins."

Martin Luther King Jr. demonstrated that the self-denial that leads to the beloved community involves disciplined hard work undertaken for the common good. Usually overlooked is his insistence that those engaged in nonviolent resistance must learn and practice with rigor specific principles and procedures if they hope to achieve its purposes. The six principles maintain that nonviolent resistance: 1) is not cowardly, 2) does not humiliate, 3) battles against forces of evil not individuals, 4) requires a willingness to suffer, 5) believes love is central, and 6) understands that the universe is built on justice.

Those accepting these principles are then to employ specific tactics that include: 1) gathering information, 2) educating a team of people devoted to finding solutions, 3) negotiating peacefully, 4) taking action using peaceful tactics such as nonviolent demonstrations, letter-writing, and

---

28. Mark 8:27–38.

29. Phil 2:5–11.

petition campaigns, and 5) working for a reconciliation that benefits both the advocate and the opposition.

King believed that loving your enemy is not idealistic thinking, but disciplined action. He felt that love's success in the contemporary world necessitated very specific programs that trained adherents to strictly follow the rules and procedures. Never before have people been trained so extensively in following proper procedures to use love as a tool against an aggressor.

A common response to King's success argues that nonviolent resistance only worked because it was employed in a society based on law and Judeo-Christian values. The article "Drop Your Weapon" challenges that position.[30] Its authors, Erica Chenoweth and Maria Stephan, report their extensive study of 323 campaigns to overthrow authoritarian regimes between 1900 and 2006. Those based on nonviolent resistance were twice as likely to succeed as violent movements in ousting tyrants and bringing democratic rule. The article noted that the successful movements enjoyed mass participation, produced regime defections, and employed flexible tactics because of careful planning, training, and coordination, features emphasized in King's program.

Forgiveness

The third feature that emerges when love is placed in the context of the Christian story is forgiveness. God's love heals the damaged creation by overcoming the violence that broke it. He creates rather than destroys, blesses rather than punishes, redeems rather than abandons.

That narrative begins in Genesis 4, where God's love is frustrated by humanity's reliance on violence. One of Cain's descendants, Lamech, typified this destructive corruption when he bragged to his two wives, "I have killed a man for wounding me, a young man for striking me." It continues to Sinai where God overcame this violence by granting his people the Torah Law that teaches fairness, "an eye for an eye, a tooth for a tooth." And it is culminated in Jesus' declaration that goes beyond fairness.

> You have heard that it was said, "An eye for an eye and a tooth for a tooth." But I say to you, do not resist an evildoer . . . . You have heard that it was said, "You shall love your neighbor and hate your enemy." But I say to you, love your enemies and pray for those

30. Chenoweth and Stephan, "Drop Your Weapon."

who persecute you, so that you may be children of your Father in heaven; for he makes his sun rise on the evil and on the good, and sends rain on the righteous and on the unrighteous.[31]

Forgiveness is not simply a transaction between two people in which one is contrite, confesses, and makes some act of satisfaction while the other absolves them of their past sins. This kind of personal penance plays its part in the Christian lifestyle, as the Lord's Prayer's "Forgive our sins as we forgive those who sin against us" makes clear. However, forgiveness also plays a far more expansive role. If love is the means by which God saves, redeems, and transforms the world, forgiveness describes love's dynamic action in this penultimate time.

Conclusion

Christian love clashes head-on with the concept of power inherent in *technique*. That power of modern technology is the thread that runs through the contemporary 24/7 news reporting. Some segments thrill us with announcements of a new cancer drug, faster computer, lifesaving surgery, self-driving car, genome sequencing, agricultural breakthrough, or cognitive study. News reporters often spontaneously respond with amazement at the achievements technology makes available. Other segments frighten us with the latest terrorist attack, drone assassination, antibiotic-resistant superbug, global warming sign, refugee crisis, cyber attack, or nuclear proliferation threat. Ironically, people constantly report that these leave them feeling powerless.

The power of technology either exhilarates or frightens us. However, human nature has not changed. People still engage in projects for the survival and enrichment of themselves and their friends as well as programs for the destruction and control of their enemies. The new ingredient is the potential to efficiently achieve their goals. Power alone is always ultimately self-defeating in an environment where power begets power.

Christian love as defined by the Scriptures and understood in the technological society by Martin Luther King Jr. offers a redemptive agent of change based on unconditional care, sacrifice, and forgiveness. Returning good for evil, its nonviolent nature offers the means to transform the present situation.

---

31. Matt 5:43–45.

Christians believe that faith, hope, and love provide meaning and purpose for their own and their community's choice of actions. If faith trusts the story that God loves the creation into being, then active love is the way that humans participate in that story. If hope believes that love is the way to the beloved community, then love is the way that humans participate in its coming. It is love that ultimately holds the world together, love that makes the world go round.

A Final Word

The longer we studied the effects of technology on faith, hope, and love, the more we became convinced that one of Christianity's greatest contributions to maintaining our humanity in this society is to provide words through which people can express their thoughts, feelings, and experiences. We also rather unexpectedly came to think that friendship is one of those words that clarifies the meaning of love in our time and place.

The primary word used with love in the past was *neighbor*. The first three Gospels depict Jesus teaching his followers to love their neighbors as themselves. The intention was clearly to spread love beyond the biological family, where it is presumed. The word implies sharing with those who are nearby but also with anyone before you in need. Although neighbor still plays a special role in Christian tradition, it has lost some of its potency in our modern global village.

This loss seems to have motivated Christians to turn to "family" in recent times. They often speak of their church as a family of families. They use the relationship between husband and wife as their primary example when discussing love, as Pope Benedict did in *Caritas Est*.[32] Again, family has been important in the Christian tradition that speaks of God loving us as a father and our loving each other as sisters and brothers.

Even so, like neighbor, family presents difficulties. The biblical community accentuates loving beyond family. It lauds Jesus' disciples for leaving their families to join his band and the first churches. Contemporary believers feel uncomfortable using the family model in light of recent demographics. Family is now reduced to the intimate nuclear unit rather than extended kinship. When used for the church, it leaves out those who elect not to marry or have children, those who prefer to live together without official license, and those who are lesbian, gay, bisexual, or transgender. On

---

32. Benedict XVI, "Encyclical Letter Deus Caritas Est."

top of all that, Christians professing supposedly family values in the public arena are regarded by many as mean-spirited reactionaries who spew hate.

A third biblical word, *friend*, might well provide a more solid foundation for examining Christian love in our time and place. In contrast to the first three Gospels, John used friendship to characterize Christian love. His Gospel builds to the Last Supper, where Jesus described our relationship with God as friendship. After washing his disciples' feet, he gave them the one commandment found in this Gospel, "Love one another as I have loved you." He then presented himself as their friend, because he had shared everything with them and was willing to give his life for their welfare.[33]

John's thoughts on friendship that were developed by some early church fathers, such as Ambrose and Augustine, culminated in the marvelous twelfth-century treatise "Spiritual Friendship," by Aelred of Rievaulx. Aelred described human friendship as a means of grace leading to eternal friendship with God. He beautifully pictured it providing a way for God to embrace humanity. He wrote that friends open their hearts to one another, sharing their deepest thoughts, their hopes and fears, their joys and sorrows. They care enough to correct one another. This sharing that takes place especially in conversation is a way to truth as well as to eternal friendship with God.

Because Aelred considered the potential for friendship to be the image of God bestowed at creation, he frequently interchanged love and friendship. At times he even proclaimed that God is friendship.

The medieval monk's definition of love made a distinction between friendship and charity. Christian friendship entailed a mutual beneficence that cannot be assumed in our relationships with those outside of the community. Nonetheless, the church must care for people outside their group just as Jesus befriended sinners, tax collectors, and even Judas who betrayed him. Paul expressed the difference when he defined love within the community as not insisting on its own way and love extended beyond it as returning good for evil. Aelred made the distinction this way:

> There is a vast difference between charity and friendship; for divine authority approves that more are to be received into the bosom of charity than into the embrace of friendship. For we are compelled by the law of charity to receive in the embrace of love not only our friends but also our enemies. But only those do we call friends to whom we can fearlessly entrust our heart and all its

---

33. John 15:12–17.

secrets; those, too, who, in turn, are bound to us by the same law of faith and security.[34]

Two of the theologians we have mentioned also champion using friendship as a model for love in our day. Ivan Illich[35] was convinced that the trust of friendship includes graceful and playful features that would allow the church to be more creative and relevant for modern personal relationships.[36] Stanley Hauerwas was speaking of this same creative freedom when he wrote, "Friendship becomes our way of life as we learn to rejoice in the presence of others."[37] He went on to describe the Christian life as based on the truthfulness with which good friends relate to one another.

Both of the sociologists we have been citing believe that our society would regain some desirable stability by promoting friendship. Luhmann believes that friendship is a "more constant and calm" form of pure relationship than contemporary marriage, which he categorizes as merely intimacy.[38] Giddens thinks friendship offers a more democratized and thus self-determinate kind of personal relationship, suitable for our time and place because it gives women and homosexual individuals roles.[39]

Above all, we think using friendship to express the meaning of love goes a long way in overcoming the self-absorption that results from discerning all through the lens of technology. We recommend that the church rediscover this part of its tradition as a complement if not a replacement of neighbor and family.

---

34. Aelred of Rievaulx, *Spiritual Friendship*, #32.
35. Illich, *The Rivers North of the Future*, 147–52.
36. Garrigos, "Hospitality Cannot be a Challenge," 135.
37. Hauerwas, *The Peaceable Kingdom*, 91–92.
38. Luhmann, *Love as Passion*, 74.
39. Giddens, *The Transformation of Intimacy*, 182.

8

Connections

MANY WORRY THAT TECHNOLOGY is destroying community. Typically they point to Robert Putnam's study in *Bowling Alone,* which claims that volunteer societies are disappearing as people stay in their homes watching television. Putnam concluded that without personal contact, people lose trust in one another and have trouble working together for the good of society.

Seemingly in contradiction to Putnam's warning, more kids today are playing team sports. However, a great change that reflects the influence of the technological society has taken place over the lifetimes of the two authors. Two generations ago, most young people engaged in pick-up games in their neighborhoods. Now youth sports are highly organized.

Forty years ago, the younger of us spent as much time as possible outside playing football and baseball and the like with the kids who lived nearby. Adults felt safe allowing their children to run around unsupervised in their neighborhoods. The lack of supervision was evident as each game began with choosing sides, teams which could change each day. Many, if not most, of the games ended in squabbles over whether plays were fair. If asked what they were doing, the kids would probably reply that they were wasting time with their friends. The adults would express something about how the kids were learning to organize their lives and take care of themselves.

Our fourteen-year-old son/grandson did not even understand the term *pick-up game* when his coach invited four teams to participate in one over Memorial Day. To him, engaging in athletics meant belonging to a house, travel, or premier version of a sport. That typically involves spending every afternoon at practice for most of the year and going to tournaments most weekends. Families commonly spend thousands of dollars each year to enroll their children in a league and to provide transportation. They effectively become hockey moms and soccer dads. If asked what they were doing, the kids would probably talk about winning the league title. Adults might state something about learning teamwork, but more likely about how to succeed in life.

These highly organized teams appear to be the kind of volunteer societies that Putnam believed are essential for building a healthy society. At the same time, they reflect just how much modern technology influences everything we do. Specialization has become so important that talented youth are expected to play only one position in only one sport year-round. Coaches are regarded as experts who will train and direct the kids. Because every aspect of the game has to be measured, statistics increasingly play a larger role. Officials are paid to supervise the game and make sure that every play is fair. The goal is clearly to win the league title. Teams are known to fall apart and not complete their schedules when this becomes impossible.

Community

When we set out to examine how the modern technological society affects faith, hope, and love, we were continually forced to consider how *technique* has changed community in our time and place. Faith's narrative is a story shared by the community, hope's vision is based on the common good of the community, and love's most simple definition is caring for all people in the community. The three theological virtues obviously inform and inspire the individual's connection to the community.

This led us to utilize the sociological distinction between local and associative communities. A local community is a group living together in the same area or neighborhood. An associative community is a group sharing a common interest, belief, activity, etc. The difference between the two most relevant for our study is the richness of their connections to place and time.

Connections to Place

Local communities are usually associated with a sense of place that a number of empirical studies have shown is important for a person's well-being.

The basic idea builds on Vanderwolk's claim that environment has a defining influence on the shared experience of people in a local community.[1]

However, that connection to place is defined differently depending on the discipline making the study. The anthropologist Setha Low spoke about place attachment, which provides people with symbolic relationships to others that provide culturally shared emotional and affective meaning to a particular space.[2] The sociologist David Hummon claimed that it is an emotional reaction to a person's environment that connects them to that locale.[3] Geographer Yi-Fu Tuan described it as a bond between people and place.[4] The psychiatrist Mindy Thompson Fullilove considered the loss of connection to place to be a major mental health disorder, as can be readily observed in displacement by events such as war, epidemics, and natural disasters.[5] Some features of the disorder are also evident in moves caused by and facilitated by technology.

You can perceive the multiple dimensions of local community in Jennifer Cross's findings, which depict the connection to place in six different types of relationships.[6] The first is the biographical, which indicates the history people have in a locality, such as being born and raised there. The second is the spiritual, which is simply the sense of belonging that one can feel with a location. Another is the ideological, which comes out of an ethical or religious sense of responsibility to a locale. The narrative involves a story or myth shared by the community, what we have been calling a common story. Another is the commodified, which lists desirable traits that people associate with a place, and the final is the dependent, which refers to the opportunities brought by features such as the kind of people and economic opportunity in the locale.

In our technological society, associative communities have largely replaced these local communities, just as organized sports have replaced neighborhood pick-up games. Associative communities bring together people with similar interests, whether that interest is playing a particular game, participating in a hobby, or engaging in business transactions. The modern forms of this kind of community began with the rise of professional

1. Vanderwolk, "Invisible Communities."
2. Low, "Critical Landscape Architecture."
3. Hummon, "Community Attachment."
4. Tuan, *Topophilia*.
5. Fullilove, "Psychiatric implications of displacement."
6. Cross, "What is Sense of Place?"

societies and the increase in topical periodicals in the latter half of the nineteenth century. Magazines enabled people separated by vast distances to link with one another.[7] Modern transportation does the same for members of an athletic squad who might live many miles from the rest of the team. Electronic communication creates even more opportunities, as people with any kind of interest whatsoever, from bird-watching to conjugating Tolkien Elvish or Klingon, can connect with others anywhere in the world.

The primary difference between local and associative communities might well be that the former are multifunctional and the latter single-functional. Local communities deal with many, if not all, aspects of the lives of those who live within them. Members share a wide range of experiences. The values that give meaning and purpose to these common experiences address the needs of a much more integrated and comprehensive understanding of life.

Because associative communities gather people for a single function, their values are limited to that activity. For example, organized athletic teams promote good sportsmanship and occupational societies advocate professional ethics. These values work for setting standards in that particular project.

A youth soccer team is clearly an associative community in which persons interact physically with one another. The new electronic communities hailed in the technological society, on the other hand, are associative communities in which the participants might never be physically present to one another at any time.

Although the church can be described as both a local and an associative community, she predominately functions as neighborhood congregations. Believers must gather face-to-face if they are to share the Word and sacraments. However, most local congregations confess their membership in the holy catholic church, which can be understood as an associative community composed of all those who share an interest in following Jesus Christ.[8]

Connections to Time

The thread running through all of these studies of local community is the importance of widespread experiences shared over an extended period of

---

7. Bledstein, *The Culture of Professionalism*.
8. Foltz and Foltz, "Religion on the Internet."

time. Members who share considerable time with each other eventually develop a common story, a narrative connecting their past, present, and future. It is more rhyme than reason, more historical than rational. Its narrative informs and inspires by providing an identity and a direction for the members of the community.

Obviously an associative community can also have a history, but it revolves around one particular activity. The actions of a youth soccer team can be inspired by its *esprit de corps*, which is largely based on remembering its past performances. However, the history that unites the team is all about soccer games.

The common story shared by a local community involves all the issues of living together for a long period of time. Its history founds a culture that gives meaning and purpose to the group. It provides standards for the good life or the good world envisaged by the community. In that fashion, it inspires trust, undergirds a justice system, and provides a foundation for making ethical decisions.[9,10]

Technique

Many in our technological society, especially politicians, economists, and academics, now speak of a global community. When they depict this as a global village, it becomes clear the implication is that it operates like a local community. The Internet is regarded as a place where people can meet. There is no need for a shared history or common story, because electronic media supposedly enable people to acknowledge and resolve their problems quickly. At the same time, the global village hardly fits our definition of an associative community. It is much more accurate to see that it is an economic system characterized by *technique*.

We have defined *technique* as the sociological phenomenon in which technology becomes the solution to all human problems. Just as scientism believes scientific methods can be used to explain everything, so in the environment of *technique* everything becomes a problem to be solved by technology. Everything is reduced to that directly related to the problem at hand.

Contrary to the popular perception that modern technology makes connections stronger by overcoming the limitations of time and space, we

9. Foltz and Foltz, "The Search for Trust."
10. Foltz and Foltz, "Technology, Religion, and Justice."

have examined the many ways it disconnects people from their communities, places, and histories. This disconnect begins by making efficiency its only standard and thereby reducing community into an artificial system that denigrates cultural beliefs, customs, and values. Local communities become obstacles when trying to solve global problems. The crisis in language and values that has resulted has increasingly forced our society to use power alone for solving its problems.

Efficiency

The goal of *technique* is using the most efficient means for getting what we want. Langdon Winner contends that technicians always respond to people raising cultural issues with "that's all well and good, but it is no way to run a railroad."[11] In the modern technological environment, efficiency always trumps culture.

Many claim Winner is not being fair. Technicians insist we have simply moved into a multicultural global community in which all beliefs, customs, and traditions are respected. However, it does not take long to realize there is a big difference between respect understood as tolerating people holding particular beliefs and permission allowing them to use those beliefs in making critical social decisions. In our modern society, an individual or group may practice any custom they want as long as they realize it has no bearing on any larger, important collective action. All traditions will be regarded as having equal worth, but none are relevant for economic or political policy. Differences cannot be allowed to bring confusion or delay to technological projects. Uniformity always trumps diversity.

This became evident when a number of states began to pass laws making sure that same-sex partners would not get the same benefits as heterosexual couples. Large corporations stepped in and demanded that the states' governors veto these laws. This was not necessarily a reflection of corporate social values so much as an efficient bureaucratic decision. Each state adopting a different policy concerning the rights of partners would create a nightmare for human resources.

---

11. Winner, *The Whale and the Reactor*, 36.

Virtual Reality

Jacques Ellul argued that this obsession with efficiency has brought on a crisis in language in which spatial images, numbers, and scientific formulae replace words in *technique*.[12] Although technicians claim that they are delivering accuracy and objectivity by overcoming the ambiguity of words, they have actually constructed a virtual reality by removing language from its real-life contexts. Images, numbers, and formulae must have context imposed upon them.

For example, the very famous picture of the marines raising the flag over Iwo Jima is a moment taken out of time. It might be infused with all sorts of feelings and values, but these have to be imposed from outside the image. Without an accompanying narrative, the picture has no meaning. Standing alone it conveys nothing about the thousands who died on that island. Indeed, the actual photo was staged as a public relations exercise to sell war bonds.

In the same manner, Matthew Brady used the new technology of photography to create staged images for his own purposes. Arriving at Gettysburg after the Civil War battle had ended, Brady placed the same few dead bodies at various places on the field. The photographs that expressed the horror of that battle went far in making Brady's reputation. However, when close examination reveals the same dead at Devil's Den as at The Bloody Angle, one realizes that the image is not historically accurate.

Likewise, anyone who ever experiences a major sporting event live knows how different it is than what you see on television. The television experience is mediated not only by the commentary of the announcer, but perhaps even more by what the technical director allows you to see. The two authors recently attended a major international soccer event. The sanitized image portrayed on the telecast shown later in no way showed the intense animosity of the fans supporting the rival teams. Nor did it show the interactions of players with the fans. Even televised images have context imposed upon them.

As images, symbols, and numbers replace words, meaningful narrative is disappearing. Public conversation is filled with slogans, commonplaces, code words, bumper stickers, and other half-truths. The meaning and purpose that a common story provided for decision-making fades in

---

12. Ellul, *The Humiliation of the Word*.

importance as words become power tools, simply used to get what you or your group wants.

Loss of Values

This in turn has led to a loss of cultural values. Thinking ethically involves considering standards and purposes that are derived from the customs, beliefs, and traditions of our culture. When we allow *technique* to degrade or extinguish these, efficiency becomes the premier, and often only, value. This leaves us with a global society better described as fragmented than pluralistic.

This situation is especially dangerous because the power of modern technology has created a perilous world, requiring courageous, innovative moral thought. If our technologies provide the power to do it, the most efficient path to having your own way is to eliminate anyone who opposes you. One reason the Nazis' final solution horrifies us is that it was perpetrated by the German people, whom most regarded as the most efficient people on earth. Any examination of the Holocaust is extremely uncomfortable because, either consciously or unconsciously, we find it conceivable that any nation might engage in genocide if it seems in its self-interest. We are terrified by the inevitable proliferation of nuclear weapons because we realize that any nation might use them. The fact that we can calmly justify our own nation's bombing of Hiroshima and Nagasaki as saving the lives of our soldiers only adds to the unspeakable dreadfulness of the violence. Again, one primary reason we are frightened by climate change is that it reveals our own unwillingness to acknowledge our obligation to care for the environment no matter what the data reveals.

At the very time that technology has created conditions demanding disciplined, ethical thought, it has also created an environment that devastates the cultures that have generated our traditional moral principles. Our inability to bring ethical thought to the problems caused by the power of modern technology has resulted in all sorts of potentially self-destructive situations.

Power

In this dangerous situation, the technological society increasingly relies on power alone to solve all of its problems. Technology is ultimately power that enables you to do what you want or to make others do what you want them to do.

Steven Lukes posited that there are three dimensions of power.[13] Direct power is the straightforward definition used by most social scientists.[14] It is the ability to make other people do what they would not normally do. Modern technology provides direct power beyond the comprehension of most individuals. The most obvious example is the vast military might of the United States that easily overwhelmed Iraq. The shock and awe tactics validated technological military power over the use of human resources in waging war. It led many to believe that we have the ability to reshape the world into one that we deem useful to us.

The epitome of direct power replacing ethical reason was the Mutually Assured Destructive (MAD) doctrine employed during the Cold War. It assumed we could threaten nuclear war to settle disputes because no one was foolish enough to start a conflict that would end up destroying both the US and the USSR. It takes little thought to realize that this cannot be an ongoing sustainable policy, as one mistake brings complete destruction.

The second dimension of power is non-decision-making, which prevents people from making certain decisions by keeping issues off the agenda. For instance, choosing to eat at a Chinese restaurant offers many choices. However, because you are at a Chinese restaurant, pizza and tacos are not options. So too the environment of the technological society limits choice. The billions of dollars spent on highway construction to facilitate automotive transportation make it highly unlikely that we will replace the car with public transportation. The cost of the quick strike force of modern military technology makes it tremendously difficult to oppose a war once it is started.

The epitome of non-decision-making power might be the NRA's commonplace, "The only way to stop a bad guy with a gun is a good guy with a gun." By refusing to acknowledge any other options, the gun lobby perpetrates our society's descent from justice system to vigilantism.

Non-decision-making obviously favors those in power and creates problems for people supporting social change. Elite groups can keep issues off the agenda and thereby maintain the status quo.[15]

---

13. Lukes, *Power.*
14. Drawn from Weber, *Economy and Society.*
15. Crenson, *The Un-Politics of Air Pollution.*

Lukes's third dimension of power is ideology. The doctrines associated with people's beliefs preclude certain actions outside the paradigm of their creeds. The easy example of ideology limiting choices is that of abortion. Pro-choice supporters can choose not to have an abortion as they have a wider option space. Pro-life supporters cannot choose to have an abortion as their ideology prevents this choice.

It is this power of ideology that has surprised technicians in our modern era. Direct power has paled when confronted by personal belief systems. For instance, military technology enabled a quick invasion of Iraq; however it has not been able to force the inhabitants to behave as the conquerors desired. Just as in Vietnam, the technological force of a giant is slowly being overwhelmed by the non-technological might of humans willing to sacrifice all for their beliefs.

The values we have associated with local and religious communities still obviously inspire many people to resist succumbing to *technique*. Sadly, our study has shown that their efforts have very often backfired. When parochial communities try to oppose the violence of technology, they usually end up resorting to direct power and making matters worse.

Connections

The critical question becomes whether it is possible to use technology in a creative and positive manner to serve the common good. Does *technique* always turn such efforts in self-serving directions? Can technology become an instrument for serving God and humanity?

Throughout this study we have advocated the position that H. Richard Niebuhr labeled "Christ the Transformer of Culture" in his classic *Christ and Culture*. Niebuhr described this relationship as a "positive and hopeful attitude toward culture" based on three theological convictions. The first is the *logos* theology found in the Gospel and First Letter of John. It proclaims Christ the Son of God has always been present creatively working in this world, even though never totally discerned.[16] Niebuhr claims this is a theme "neither overpowered by nor overpowering the idea of atonement."[17] The crucifixion is simply the critical creative act of the *logos*. In the resurrection,

---

16. John 1:1–18.
17. Niebuhr, *Christ and Culture*, 192.

the Risen Christ invites his followers to join this redeeming work of love now.[18]

The second conviction is Paul's understanding of biblical Powers as perverted and corrupted goods. Being fundamentally good, they can be redeemed and restored to their proper functions. Niebuhr maintains this means that "The problem of culture is therefore the problem of its conversion not of its replacement by a new creation; though the conversion is so radical that it amounts to a kind of rebirth."[19] And the third conviction is that "to God all things are possible in history that is fundamentally not a course of merely human events but always a dramatic interaction between God and men."[20]

We have identified technology as a dysfunctional biblical Power. For that matter, we have described the institutional church and religion in general as biblical Powers. It is the Son of God, the *logos*, not the institutional church or Christianity understood as a religion in society, that saves the world. The risen Christ is restoring all Powers to their proper roles. That means he operates through human institutions but also beyond them through the human community and the Christian community that cannot be measured sociologically. Theologians sometimes characterized the latter as the invisible church.

We have also described Niebuhr's dramatic interaction of God and humanity as a public conversation taking place beyond that which sociology can measure. The Christian voice in that conversation can be a means of grace by which the risen Christ enriches our lives. From this perspective Martin Luther King Jr.'s "I Have a Dream" speech could be regarded as a political as well as a religious vision of the future. The dream might not be realized fully until Christ comes back; however, it still can be used politically if it is not identified with specific governmental programs.

The Word that the church speaks in the community conversation is a means of grace simply by forcing the larger community to consider humanity's deep relationships with our environment, locality, historical situation, and community. Beyond that, however, the Christian voice reminds the community of life's mystery and ambiguity as it champions the totality of life and the singularity of every person and thing.

---

18. John 22.
19. Niebuhr, *Christ and Culture*, 194.
20. Niebuhr, *Christ and Culture*, 191–94.

Connections

Connection to Nature

Technique's disconnect from nature becomes clear in Kurzweil's technological expectation that cannot wait for the chance to live in a machine-centered environment. Because he and his school believe that nature imposes limits on humanity, they look forward to the Singularity when humans can soar into a future defined by all-powerful machine intelligence.

President Clinton's optimism is a perfect example of how *technique* reduces nature to a resource. He seems to be arguing for sustainable technologies that preserve nature. However, his bottom line always insists that green technologies will provide economic prosperity. The suspicion remains that he really supports corporate power and large-scale green industries that produce profit for the privileged but do little to connect all people to their environment.

One way that contemporary culture can overcome this disconnect and reductionism is simply by following the data of modern science. Its findings report the interrelatedness of all things. A change in one part of the cosmos affects in some ways every other part. A narrative built on those discoveries would acknowledge that our relationship with nature is so mutually advantageous that the preservation of the environment is a given. Caring for the environment is not only about our surviving or having an ongoing supply of fuel, but even more about living in harmony with our surroundings. That kind of narrative, in which nature is a reciprocal reality rather than a resource, would provide our communities with a giant step forward in tackling climate change.

The Christian community provides all sorts of resources in the biblical stories that appreciate humanity's connections with nature. Faith's story begins with God the Father creating and caring for the universe. One of hope's visions is an ecological city in which the land flourishes. The lifestyle of love includes observing the Torah's call for giving special attention to caring for the land and animals. The Scriptures from beginning to end see God's benevolence reflected in his creation. A careful telling of this story would provide an enriched understanding of the order that scientific analysis reads only as indifference.

Connection to Place

President Clinton is also a champion for technology breaking humanity's connections to place. He celebrates the breaking down of borders as that facilitates people and ideas gathering together in a homogenous world. He hails every advance in electronic media as a step forward in overcoming the limitations of physical location. He speaks glowingly of the global community.

Although we have continually agreed that these technological advances have brought benefits to humanity, we have also noted significant disadvantages. With the touch of a button we can buy Christmas presents made in China, but we cannot build meaningful personal relationships with the strangers who made them or filled our electronic orders. We can easily raise money for people starving in Africa while being diverted from families in our own locale who are unable to place food on their tables. We can know almost instantaneously about a disaster happening on the other side of the globe without being aware of our next-door neighbor's troubles. Although electronic media enable us to contact people on the other side of the globe, they also contribute to the loss of our local cultures.

We cited a number of studies showing that a people's culture is based on sharing a multitude of experiences in a common place. Such a community thrives on unique individuals engaging with one another. A global society, on the other hand, is a mass in which everybody is the same and nobody is special. Because of this anonymity, we prefer to speak of it as a global system. In fact, in many ways it is really an economic system, as it reduces all to the needs of the commercial market.

Cultural communities would do well to remember that place plays a special role in bringing their people together. One of their primary functions is to provide identity, meaning, and purpose for their members. That means they should carefully resist succumbing completely to the tremendous demands bombarding them constantly to concentrate on multicultural studies. Priority is better given to remembering the narratives that made their people who they are, and this involves how their customs and traditions developed from their sense of place.

Christian communities again have many resources in biblical narratives. Faith's stories were always based on historical events in specific localities. The exodus was linked to the Hebrews enslavement in Egypt. All the following events in the history of salvation were identified with places that are part of their meaning. Even the resurrection was colored by its occurring in Jerusalem, where the temple and political capital were located. Hope's visions include the safety of people's homes, the prospering of their lands, and the health of their surroundings. Love's actions give priority to the needy person standing before you. God's presence or nearness is the central feature of every proclamation of the Gospel message.

Connection to Time

Technology also disconnects us from past and future by focusing our attention on the immediate event. Everything is analyzed as a physical structure that pretty much endures as it is, rather than history where nothing is ever the same again. This makes for a culture of now, in which all is short-term and instant gratification as each person pursues their own version of happiness. The only meaning of the past is the information it contributes to the solution of the immediate problem at hand. The only purpose in the future is the next technological advance that will provide more opportunity to pursue one's personal happiness.

By focusing on the present problem, technicians are inclined to spin the past to support their positions. Along these same lines, they present projects that support their own or their group's priorities as rational ways to plan for the future. Preserving the *status quo* is a major goal for the chief benefactors of technology.

Providing a sense of self is one of any culture's major functions. The meaning it gives to an individual's life is based primarily on wisdom inherited from its community's past. The purpose it uses to inform an individual's actions is bound up with visions of the future shared by its members. A healthy culture depends on engaging the past and the future. Mondaugen's Law asserts that "Personal density . . . is directly proportional to temporal bandwidth," meaning that the depth of the self depends on to what extent its present is influenced by the past and future.[21]

Again, faith, hope, and love enhance that connection with time for Christians. Faith trusts the story of salvation whose genesis lies deep in the past, hope relies on the promises that story makes about the future that might be far ahead, and together they inspire and inform the love that defines Christian life in the present. The Christian gospel is a historical narrative that remembers God's actions in the past and awaits the fulfillment of his promises in the future. It is always proclaimed in the context of time.

---

21. Mendelson, "In the Depths of the Digital Age."

Connection with Community

Technique fosters the radical individualism that plagues our society. Unable to establish a common story or common good, it promises to provide many, many options so that each individual can have whatever they want. The idea of intimacy discussed in the love chapter is a good example of this disconnect from community. Retreating into an intimate relationship insulates the couple from outside issues, isolating them from others that could share their lives.

Our study repeatedly questioned whether electronic media could really provide community. The disembodied nature of online gatherings eliminates the vulnerability that characterizes the fullness of community. The Web, with its vast nonhierarchical nature, yields at best only a mass. That is not to say that caring friendships cannot be maintained and sustained electronically, but simply that in order to be complete, they cannot be entirely online. We illustrated this by pointing to the difference in proclaiming "I love you" in person or online. When physically present, the speakers make themselves available far more than they are able to do electronically. For these reasons, we refrain from speaking of an electronic community, just as we restrain ourselves from using the term for the global system.

Cultural communities can certainly challenge the radical individualism of *technique*. To speak of a self-made or contained individual is hardly reasonable in our modern society where every person is extremely dependent on others for their economic, political, social, ethical, and spiritual needs. We suggested that promoting friendship might have great potential for modern communities when many traditional forms of personal relationship have been weakened. It is difficult to base culture on family when so many now elect to remain single or to be childless if married. Friendship offers a more inclusive relationship that overcomes the self-absorption of individualism but also avoids the exclusion of those without family.

By nature, the church is a community that shares her gifts rather than a gathering of individuals each seeking their own goals. Faith is based on the story of that community, hope offers a vision of all people gathered into that community, and love expresses the actions making up the lifestyle of that community. The church also has a rich ancient tradition that proclaimed Christian friendship. From John the evangelist to Dr. Martin Luther King Jr., many theologians have claimed that the goal of the Christian community is eventually to make all enemies friends.

CONNECTIONS

Conclusions

When examining the connections essential for a healthy community, it quickly becomes apparent that a great deal of their richness is their interaction. You begin writing about one of them and quickly find yourself including characteristics of the others. You cannot describe nature without mentioning place. It is impossible to explain a sense of place without mentioning its importance for community. You think you are explaining time and end up pairing it with place. Any analysis of community includes how it is informed by all three of the other connections.

We found the same when we tried to analyze faith, hope, and love as separate virtues. It is impossible to study one without speaking of the others. Their interaction is essential to their function. That is especially significant if you see their role as providing the ingredients for Christian decision-making. From that perspective, faith and hope inform and inspire love.

Of course, any analysis is artificial in the sense that it separates from one another parts that interact in real life. That observation takes us back to Jacques Ellul's observation that "Anyone wishing to save humanity today must first of all save the word."[22] It is language that makes the connections for both culture and religion. It makes common sense from the kaleidoscope of sense experiences we receive from nature. It creates a common narrative from the experiences we share with others in our locality. It connects the past and future with our present time. And finally, it enables us to communicate in depth with others in our communities.

At the same time, the ambiguity of words reminds us of the uncertainty of any of our analyses of reality. We best maintain a grasp on an actual situation in the back and forth, give and take of an ongoing conversation.

As our study of faith, hope, and love indicated, language is critical for the Christian message. Language not only creates a common world in which people can understand one another, it also enables the divine-human relationship to thrive. Believers can only indicate what they mean by God with words. They can best characterize the history of salvation reported in the Bible as an ongoing conversation. We shall take a final look at what this means for the present Christian community in the next and last chapter.

---

22. Ellul, *The Humiliation of the Word*, 254.

9

So What?

THE YOUNGER AUTHOR HAD a professor in grad school who always asked the question "So what?" when colleagues gave a lecture or a student made a presentation. Some took it as a rude comment, but in reality it is a very pertinent question for those who think that academic exercises should have some relevance in the real world. In this chapter, we hope to answer "So what?" in regard to our work.

Our intention is primarily to draw attention to how modern technology is changing the very fabric of our culture. We wanted to do this by examining how technology is morphing the words and concepts basic for both civil society and the church. Of course, we were most concerned in this study with how modern technology has affected the three theological virtues of faith, hope, and love.

Central to our goal was pointing out the role of *technique*, which we defined as the environment that believes technology solves all human problems. As modern technology has created a global economic system, it has made irrelevant the customs, practices, and beliefs of traditional cultures. By default, the values of *technique*, especially efficiency, have replaced those of Christianity as standards for Western civilization.

Awareness

We have no desire to return to a past without modern technology. In fact, we love digital music and our various electronic devices. We use electronic media to contact friends, family, and colleagues all around the world. And

So What?

we have benefited greatly from medical technology. Plus, we never could have written this book without the ability to interact via various media.

We do hope we can incite people to pay more attention to the changes modern technology is making to the way we live. Technological change has been so relentlessly speedy that people rarely are able to assess its effects. Scholars and ordinary citizens give passing mention to how much technology has affected everything we do and then go on to discuss other issues at length. Few have examined deeply what the impacts are.

One of the most threatening is how much *technique* presently dominates our decision-making. Most people think of technology as simply the tools and particular technologies that enable us to do what we want. They assume we are continually making choices about which tools we shall use and how we shall use them. This mind-set overlooks how much the environment created by modern technology has increasingly taken decision-making away from us.

Technique has pretty much destroyed the familiarity that engendered the trust at the heart of decision-making in traditional societies. Personal decisions are now confined to rational choices that only really work in very limited, mostly economic, situations. Citizens are expected to leave societal decisions to the workings of technological systems and those who maintain them. *Technique* replaces the wisdom of the past. The Kennedy speech we examined in the first chapter revealed how much control it has over governmental decisions. Although *technique* was around prior to that talk, Kennedy heralded its dominance on the world stage.

Decision-Making

Our second goal is to inspire people to engage in making decisions about how technology is used. Some of our friends in technological studies question if it is realistic to speak of making decisions about appropriate technologies. They think the all-encompassing self-serving environment of *technique* has created a system beyond human intervention. The power of our technologies forces us to develop more and more, faster and faster, newer and newer gadgets and systems.

Other friends think momentous decisions are still being made by corporate executives who intentionally seek to exclude the input of other people. These business leaders argue that any kind of government interference that well might represent the public voice hinders necessary technical development. So much time and money is needed for research and testing that there is no place for anyone but those involved to consider beginning or continuing projects. In reality, this has come to mean that those concerned with economic profit rather than those pursuing the common good or even those involved in the technology itself are making decisions for everyone else. Because common people and their representatives are never offered a significant voice, changes are imposed on society without its consent. Citizens are expected to passively accept whatever happens.

We ourselves see no reason to be so cynical, fatalistic, or indifferent; however, we acknowledge that creative participation is no easy matter. Way back in 1973, E. F. Schumacher claimed that it would mean a complete reversal of our thinking. The title of his book, *Small is Beautiful*, indicates the kind of radically different priorities he thought necessary. The chapter on an economic system based on Buddhism is especially interesting for our purposes. More recently, in 2010, John McKnight and Peter Block published *The Abundant Community: Awakening the Power of Families and Neighborhoods*. Again, the title expresses their thesis that building a bountiful society will mean changing direction. Rather than glorifying the benefits of a global economic system, it will appreciate how much the good life depends on the gifts shared in small local groups.

We have suggested that one way to do this might be make sure your voice is heard in the ongoing public conversation about the appropriateness of particular technologies. Although this conversation is mighty hard to detect in the modern technological society, there is an everyday exchange of opinions that constantly goes on all around us. The media, academia, and government affect it, but it also influences them. Its power is evident when it erupts into view during public outcries about corporate policies such as the price of medical supplies. If enough citizens express outrage in these isolated incidents, businesses quickly make changes.

Our background is Pennsylvania Dutch, so we immediately think of the Amish. Contrary to public opinion, this religious community is not anti-technology. When you visit their territories, you realize that they use a number of modern technological devices. However, before they accept a new one, their bishops determine whether it will interfere with their families or faith. If you live in their neighborhoods, you realize that this has created a questionable situation where the sect retreats into isolated communities to practice their way of life, but emerges to take advantage of the modern technology others provide. For instance, you often find Amish people who advocate ending education at eighth grade utilizing the skills of highly educated doctors in the most up-to-date hospitals.

Our challenge is to promote a responsible conversation that goes beyond such parochial values. President Obama called for this in the commencement speech to which we referred in the first chapter. He argued that society needs to start questioning its non-reflective adoption of all technology. Like the Amish, he was accused of being anti-technology and asking people to give up their technological devices. However, he was simply suggesting that society would be better off if it began to actively choose which types of technology it accepted.

The Humanities

The president was calling for the academic community, especially faculty in the liberal arts, to provide values that would help us make appropriate decisions about technology. In the past, the humanities and the arts played that role by supplying canons and standards. Dealing with life in all its messiness, they tried to bring order out of chaos by preserving the wisdom of the past while at the same time providing the cutting edge for the future.

At present, the humanities, like everything else, must resist the temptations of *technique*. They are increasingly called to teach vocational skills rather than critical thinking. Multicultural studies are advocated as realistic contemporary foundations for human values. Respect for diversity is championed over dealing with the intentions of authors, making distinctions of truth and falsehood, or discriminating between relevance and noise. Some have even begun practicing a form of digital humanity that relies on computers to detect similarities and differences in vast quantities of data, thereby establishing patterns of use rather than standards of quality.

As the expectation for finding meaning and purpose for culture seems to recede, academic departments retreat into their own specialties. Helpful as this might be for making advances in their own fields, it hardly supplies the values that President Obama is seeking. Hopefully, interdisciplinary conversations and projects might develop that consciously work toward finding common goods.

Choosing how to use technology appropriately is a moral decision that classically would involve the cardinal virtues of prudence, temperance, fortitude, and justice. Contrary to the common practice of studying each separately as habits or dispositions that incline a person to do good and avoid evil, we believe it is helpful to think of their interaction as providing resources for decision-making. Prudence, temperance, and fortitude are instrumental to making just decisions and performing just actions. Because the moral virtues depend on human reasoning, they of course can be misdirected for personal advantage rather than for the common good.

Christianity

The church has maintained that the theological virtues correct this misdirection by bringing God into the conversation. The divine grace inherent in faith, hope, and love directs the moral virtues on constructive paths. Just as the function of the moral virtues is to discern and promote just actions, so faith and hope inform and inspire loving actions.

We have portrayed Christian salvation as being all about God delivering humanity and creation from self-destruction. The theological virtues enable humans to discern what God is doing in the world so that they can join in on the divine project. Faith proclaims the story of God's unconditional promise to save the world and hope reveals the vision of the future emanating from that promise. The Christian makes loving decisions based on that proclamation and vision.

The interaction of faith, hope, and love also makes clear the importance of language. Their interchange presents the Christian story as a historical narrative rather than a systematic theology. We argued that this story can best be characterized as an ongoing conversation in which God is the great speaker who always relates to humans with nonviolent words. God is a word event. He comes to us in words and the only way we can share him is in words.

However, in order to have a voice with any integrity in the public conversation, the church must first disentangle Christian words from the way society has appropriated them for its own use. She will have nothing of significance to say unless she restores words like faith, hope, and love to their proper contexts in the Christian story. Recovering the proper meaning of words is an essential part of getting Principalities, Powers, and Authorities to function appropriately.

Finally, one of the primary benefits of reviving Christian words is the realism they bring. We constantly found scholars and citizens acknowledging the artificial world of virtual reality and yearning for a more honest and caring community. They usually fell into one of two groups. The first was fatalistic about any potential for change. The second thought hope lay in overcoming human limitations, ignorance, error, and accident. Seldom were any willing to speak of evil or confront the downright sin that corrupts human endeavors.

As soon as you earnestly begin using faith, hope, and love in their traditional roles, you find yourself confronted with the church's rich understanding of repentance and forgiveness. *Technique* tries to free itself from the parts of the past that hinder creatively building a future by naively ignoring them or by attempting to overpower them with something bigger, faster, and newer. In the context of the theological virtues, repentance is first to admit that you are willfully refusing to act in love, second to rethink what you are doing, and third to change your actions. This dynamic process enables forgiveness to free us from the parts of the past that shackle us by overcoming evil with good. And it enables us to retain the parts that could contribute to a positive future by building on them in love.

The theological virtues confront the reality of sin and evil that technological progress cannot overcome. A correct understanding of faith and hope informs and inspires the sacrificial love that is willing to deny self in order to participate with God in building the beloved community.

Bibliography

Aelred of Rievaulx. *Spiritual Friendship*. Collegeville, MN: Cistercian, 2010.
Attridge, Harold W. "From the Dean's Desk." *Reflections*, vol. 98, no. 2 (Fall 2011) 2.
Auden, W. H. "For the Time Being." In *Religious Drama 1: Five Plays*, edited by Marvil Halverson, 11–68. New York: Meridian, 1957.
Augustine. *Augustine Catechism: Enchiridion on Faith Hope and Charity*. The Augustine Series Book 1. Hyde Park, NY: New City, 2008.
———. *Confessions*. Translated by Henry Chadwick. Oxford: Oxford University Press, 2008.
Benedict XVI. "Encyclical Letter Deus Caritas Est." Vatican, December 25, 2005. http://w2.vatican.va/content/benedict-xvi/en/encyclicals/documents/hf_ben-xvi_enc_20051225_deus-caritas-est.html.
———. "Encyclical Letter Spe Salvi." Vatican, November 30, 2007. http://w2.vatican.va/content/benedict-xvi/en/encyclicals/documents/hf_ben-xvi_enc_20071130_spe-salvi.html.
Bezjian-Avery, A. A., et al. "New Media Interactive Advertising Vs. Traditional Advertising." *Journal of Advertising Research*, vol. 38, no. 4 (1998) 23–32.
Bledstein, Burton. *The Culture of Professionalism: The Middle Class and the Development of Higher Education in America*. New York: W. W. Norton & Company, 1978.
Bok, Sissela. *Lying: Moral Choice in Public and Private Life*. New York: Pantheon, 1978.
Borgmann, Albert. *Holding on to Reality: The Nature of Technology at the Turn of the Millennium*. Chicago: University of Chicago Press, 2000.
———. *Technology and the Character of Contemporary Life: A Philosophical Inquiry*. Chicago: University of Chicago Press, 1984.
Brown, Peter. *Through the Eye of a Needle: Wealth, the Fall of Rome, and the Making of Christianity in the West, 350–550 AD*. Princeton, NJ: Princeton University Press, 2012.
Brunner, Emil. *Faith, Hope, and Love*. Philadelphia: Westminster, 1956.
Buber, Martin. *I and Thou*. Translated by Ronald Smith. New York: Scribner, 2000.
Campus Crusade. "How to Know God." 2014. https://www.cru.org/how-to-know-god/would-you-like-to-know-god-personally.html.
Carr, Nicholas. *The Shallows: What the Internet Is Doing to Our Brains*. New York: W. W. Norton & Company, 2010.
Cassirer, Ernst. *Language and Myth*. New York: Dover, 1953.

Bibliography

Chenoweth, Erica, and Maria J. Stephan. "Drop Your Weapon: When and Why Civil Resistance Works." *Foreign Affairs*, vol. 93, no. 3 (July/August 2014) 94–106.

Chomsky, Noam. *On Language*. New York: New, 1998.

Clinton, William. "The Case for Optimism." *Time*, October 1, 2012. http://content.time.com/time/magazine/article/0,9171,2125031-1,00.html.

———. "National Nanotechnology Initiative: Leading to the Next Industrial Revolution." White House: Office of the Press Secretary, January 2, 2000. http://clinton4.nara.gov/WH/New/html/20000121_4.html.

Coffin, William Sloane. *Credo*. Louisville: Westminster John Knox, 2003.

Collins, Francis. *The Language of God: A Scientist Presents Evidence for Belief*. New York: Free, 2006.

Copeland, Kenneth. *Kenneth Copeland Ministries*. http://www.kcm.org.

Crawford, Matthew B. *The World Beyond Your Head: On Becoming an Individual in an Age of Distraction*. New York: Farrar, Straus, and Giroux, 2015.

Crenson, Matthew A. *The Un-Politics of Air Pollution: A Study of Non-Decisionmaking in the Cities*. Baltimore: John Hopkins University Press, 1971.

Cross, Jennifer E. "What is Sense of Place?" Prepared for the twelfth Headwaters Conference, Western State College, Irvine, California, November 2–4, 2001.

Dostoyevsky, Fyodor. *The Brothers Karamazov*. Translated by Constance Garnett. New York: Modern Library, 1950.

Dreyfus, Hubert L. *On the Internet*. London: Routledge, 2001.

Eliot, T. S. *The Complete Poems and Plays: 1909–1950*. New York: Harcourt, Brace, and Company, 1952.

Ellingson, Stephen. *The Megachurch and the Mainline: Remaking Religious Tradition in the Twenty-First Century*. Chicago: University of Chicago Press, 2007.

Ellul, Jacques. *A Critique of the New Commonplaces*. Translated by Helen Weaver. New York: Alfred A. Knopf, 1968.

———. *On Freedom, Love, and Power*. Edited and Translated by Willem H. Vanderburg. Toronto: University of Toronto Press, 2010.

———. *The Humiliation of the Word*. Translated by Joyce Hanks. Grand Rapids: Eerdmans, 1985.

———. *Living Faith: Belief and Doubt in a Perilous World*. Translated by Peter Heinegg. San Francisco: Harper and Row, 1983.

———. *Propaganda: The Formation of Men's Attitudes*. Translated by Konrad Kellen and Jean Lerner. New York: Alfred A. Knopf, 1965.

———. *The Technological Bluff*. Translated by Geoffrey W. Bromiley. Grand Rapids: Eerdmans, 1990.

———. *The Technological Society*. Translated by John Wilkinson. New York: Vintage, 1964.

Erikson, Erik. *Identity: Youth and Crisis*. New York: W. W. Norton and Company, 1968.

Falwell, Jerry, and Pat Robertson. "You Helped This Happen." Transcript of September 12, 2001 edition of *The 700 Club*. http://beliefnet.com/faiths/christianity/2001/09/you-helped-this-happen.aspx.

Ferber, Paul, et al. "The Internet and Participation: State Legislature Websites and the Many Definitions of Interactivity." *Bulletin of Science, Technology & Society*, vol. 25, no. 1 (2005) 85–93.

Foltz, Franz A. "Conception and Contraception: The Lutheran and Roman Catholic Positions." Unpublished paper from April 28, 1986.

Bibliography

Foltz, Franz, and Frederick Foltz. "Charity in a Technological Society: From Alms to Corporate Culture." *Bulletin of Science, Technology, and Society,* vol. 30, no. 2 (April 2010) 96–102.

———. "Religion on the Internet: Community and Virtual Existence." *Bulletin of Science, Technology, and Society,* vol. 23, no. 4 (August 2003) 321–30.

———. "The Search for Trust: Technology, Religion, and Society's Dis-ease." *Bulletin of Science, Technology, and Society,* vol. 25, no. 2 (April 2005) 115–28.

———. "Technology, Religion, and Justice: The Problems of Disembedded and Disembodied Law." *Bulletin of Science, Technology and Society,* vol. 26, no. 6 (2006) 463–71.

Francis. "Encyclical Letter Lumen Fidei." Vatican, June 29, 2013. http://w2.vatican.va/content/francesco/en/encyclicals/documents/papa-francesco_20130629_enciclica-lumen-fidei.html.

Frankfurt, Harry. *On Bullshit*. Princeton, NJ: Princeton University Press, 2005.

Fukuyama, Francis. *Trust: The Social Virtues and the Creation of Prosperity*. New York: Free, 1995.

Fullilove, Mindy Thompson. "Psychiatric implications of displacement: Contributions from the psychology of place." *The American Journal of Psychiatry,* vol. 153, no. 12 (December 1996) 1516–23.

Garrigos, Alfons. "Hospitality Cannot be a Challenge: A Collective Reflection." In *The Challenges of Ivan Illich*, edited by Lee Hoinacki and Carl Mitcham, 113–26. Albany, NY: State University of New York Press, 2002.

Gibson, David. "'Protestant Ethic' still sways dreams of wealth." *The Christian Century*. September, 2011. https://www.christiancentury.org/article/2011-09/protestant-ethic-still-sways-dreams-wealth.

Giddens, Anthony. *The Consequences of Modernity*. Stanford, CA: Stanford University Press, 1990.

———. *Modernity and Self-Identity: Self and Society in the Late Modern Age*. Stanford, CA: Stanford University Press, 1991.

———. *The Transformation of Intimacy: Sexuality, Love, and Eroticism in Modern Societies*. Stanford, CA: Stanford University Press, 1992.

Grossman, Lev. "2045: The Year Man Becomes Immortal." *Time,* February 10, 2011. http://content.time.com/time/magazine/article/0,9171,2048290,00.html.

Ha, Louisa, and Lincoln James. "Interactivity reexamined: A baseline analysis of early business web sites." *Journal of Broadcasting & Electronic Media,* vol. 42, no. 4 (1998) 457–74.

Haeckel, S. H. "About the nature and future of interactive marketing." *Journal of Interactive Marketing,* vol. 12, no.1 (1998) 63–71.

Hall, Douglas John. *The Cross in Our Context: Jesus and the Suffering World*. Minneapolis: Fortress, 2003.

Hardin, Russell. *Trust and Trustworthiness*. Russell Sage Foundation Series on Trust vol. 4. New York: Russell Sage Foundation, 2002.

Hart, David Bentley. *The Doors of the Sea: Where Was God in the Tsunami?* Kindle ed. Grand Rapids: Eerdmans, 2005.

Hauerwas, Stanley. *The Peaceable Kingdom*. Notre Dame, IN: University of Notre Dame Press, 1983.

———. *With the Grain of the Universe: The Church's Witness and Natural Theology*. Grand Rapids: Brazos, 2001.

BIBLIOGRAPHY

Hauerwas, Stanley, et al. "Ethics in our time: A conversation on Christian social witness." *The Christian Century.* September 27, 2000. https://www.christiancentury.org/article//ethics-our-time.

Heeter, Carrie. "Implications of New Interactive Technologies for Conceptualizing Communication." In *Media Use in the Information Age: Emerging Patterns of Adoption and Computer Use,* edited by Jennings Bryant and Jerry Salvaggio, 217–35. Hillsdale, NJ: L. Erlbaum Associates, 1989.

Hefner, Philip J. *The Human Factor: Evolution, Culture, and Religion.* Minneapolis: Fortress, 1993.

Hooghe, Marc, and Dietlind Stolle. "Introduction." In *Generating Social Capital: Civil Society and Institutions in Comparative Perspective,* edited by Marc Hooghe and Dietlind Stolle, 1–18. New York: Palgrave Macmillan, 2003.

Hummon, David M. "Community Attachment: Local Sentiment and Sense of Place." In *Place Attachment,* edited by Irwin Altman and Setha Low, 253–78. New York: Plenumf, 1992.

Illich, Ivan. "To Honor Jacques Ellul." Based on an address given at Bordeaux, November 13, 1993. http://www.davidtinapple.com/illich/1993_honor_ellul.PDF.

———. "The Rebirth of Epimethean Man." In *Deschooling Society,* 151–68. New ed. Open Forum Series. London: Marion Boyars, 2000.

———. *The Rivers North of the Future: The Testament of Ivan Illich as told to David Cayley.* Toronto: House of Anansi, 2005.

———. *In the Vineyard of the Text: A Commentary to Hugh's Didascalicon.* Chicago: University of Chicago Press, 1996.

Illich, Ivan, and Barry Sanders. *ABC: The Alphabetization of the Popular Mind.* 1st Vintage Books ed. New York: Vintage, 1989.

Jenson, Robert W. "The Church and Mass Electronic Media: The Hermeneutical Problem." In *Essays in Theology of Culture,* edited by Robert W. Jenson, 156–62. Grand Rapids: Eerdmans, 1995.

———. "How the World Lost its Story." *First Things,* vol. 36 (October 1993) 19–24.

———. *The Knowledge of Things Hoped For.* Oxford: Oxford University Press, 1969.

———. *A Large Catechism.* Delhi, NY: American Lutheran Publicity Bureau, 2013.

———. *Story and Promise: A Brief Theology of the Gospel About Jesus.* Philadelphia: Fortress, 1973.

Kennedy, John F. "Commencement Address at Yale." Speech, New Haven, Connecticut, June 11, 1962. http://www.presidency.ucsb.edu/ws/?pid=29661.

King, Martin Luther, Jr. "I Have a Dream." Speech, Washington, DC, August 28, 1963. http://www.let.rug.nl/usa/documents/1951-/martin-luther-kings-i-have-a-dream-speech-august-28-1963.php.

———. "The King Philosophy." *The King Center.* http://www.thekingcenter.org/king-philosophy.

———. "Loving Your Enemies." In *Strength to Love,* 43–52. Minneapolis: Fortress, 1963.

Kiousis, Spiro. "Broadening the boundaries of interactivity: A concept explication." Paper read at Association for Education in Journalism and Mass Communication Annual Conference, New Orleans, August 1999.

Kropp, Paul. *The Reading Solution: Make Your Child a Reader for Life.* Toronto: Random House of Canada, 1993.

Kurzweil, Ray. *The Age of Spiritual Machines: When Computers Exceed Human Intelligence.* New York: Penguin, 1999.

Bibliography

LaHaye, Tim, and Jerry B. Jenkins. *Left Behind: A Novel of the Earth's Last Days*. Left Behind 1. Carol Stream, IL: Tyndale, 1995.

Lerner, Alan Jay, and Frederick Loewe. *My Fair Lady: A Musical Play in Two Acts*. Based on *Pygmalion*, by George Bernard Shaw. New York: Doward-McCann, 1956.

Lindbeck, George A. *The Nature of Doctrine: Religion and Theology in a Postliberal Age*. Philadelphia: Westminster John Knox, 1984.

Lindberg, Carter. *Beyond Charity: Reformation Initiatives for the Poor*. Minneapolis: Fortress, 1993.

Low, Setha. "Critical Landscape Architecture." *Landscape Journal*, vol. 11 (1992) 172–73.

Luhmann, Niklas. "Familiarity, Confidence, Trust: Problems and Alternatives." In *Trust: Making and Breaking Cooperative Relations*, edited by D. Gambetta, 94–107. Electronic Edition. Department of Sociology, University of Oxford, 2000. https://www.sociology.ox.ac.uk/papers/luhmann94-107.pdf.

———. *Love as Passion: The Codification of Intimacy*. Stanford, CA: Stanford University Press, 1998.

Lukes, Steven. *Power: A Radical View*. New York: Macmillan, 1974.

MacIntyre, Alasdair. *After Virtue*. Notre Dame, IN: University of Notre Dame Press, 1984.

Mansbridge, Jane. "Altruistic Trust." In *Democracy and Trust*, edited by Mark Warren, 290–309. Cambridge: Cambridge University Press, 1999.

McCasland, S. "Man, Nature of." In *The Interpreter's Dictionary of the Bible*, edited by George Buttrick. Vol. 3. Nashville: Abingdon, 1962.

McGovern, G. "The Myth of Interactivity on the Internet." *New Thinking Newsletter*, March 18, 2002. http://www.gerrymcgovern.com/nt_2002_03_18_interactivity.htm.

McKibben, Bill. *The End of Nature*. New York: Random House, 2006.

McKnight, John, and Peter Block. *The Abundant Community: Awakening the Power of Families and Neighborhoods*. San Francisco: Berrett-Koehler, 2010.

McLuhan, Marshall. *Understanding Media: The Extensions of Man*. New York: Signet, 1964.

McPherson, Miller, et al. "Social Isolation in America: Changes in Core Discussion Networks over Two Decades." *American Sociology Review*, vol. 71, no. 3 (June 2006) 353–75.

Mendelson, Edward. "In the Depths of the Digital Age." *New York Review of Books*, vol. 63, no. 11 (June 23, 2016). http://www.nybooks.com/articles/2016/06/23/depths-of-the-digital-age/.

Miller, Lisa. "The Trans-Everything CEO." *New York Magazine*, September 8, 2014. http://nymag.com/news/features/martine-rothblatt-transgender-ceo/.

Murphy, Nancey. "Nonreductive Physicalism: Philosophical Issues." In *Whatever Happened to the Human Soul? Scientific and Theological Portraits of Human Nature*, edited by Nancy Murphy et al., 127–48. Minneapolis: Fortress, 1998.

Nicholas of Cusa. *Nicholas of Cusa: Selected Spiritual Writings*. Translated by H. Lawrence Bond. New York: Paulist, 1997.

Niebuhr, H. Richard. *Christ and Culture*. Harper Torch Books. New York: Harper and Brothers, 1951.

———. *Radical Monotheism and Western Culture*. Louisville: Westminster John Knox, 1960.

———. *The Responsible Self: An Essay on Christian Morals*. Louisville: Westminster John Knox, 1999.

Bibliography

Noble, David. *The Religion of Technology: The Divinity of Man and the Spirit of Technology*. New York: Penguin, 1999.

Nordvall, Robert. Personal correspondence, October 29, 2011.

Obama, Barak. "Commencement Speech at Hampton College." Speech, Hampton, Virginia, 2010. http://time.com/4340815/obama-commencement-%20speech-transcript-hampton-university/.

Orwell, George. *Nineteen Eighty-Four*. New York: Harcourt Brace and Co, 1949.

Osteen, Joel. *Joel Osteen Ministries*. http://joelosteen.lakewood.cc/site/PageServer?pagename=JOM_homepage.

Peale, Norman Vincent. *The Power of Positive Thinking*. New York: Ballantine, 1996.

Pew. "U.S. Public Becoming Less Religious." *2014 U.S. Religious Landscape Study*. Pew Research. November 3, 2015. http://www.pewforum.org/2015/11/03/u-s-public-becoming-less-religious/.

Pieper, Josef. *Faith, Hope, Love*. San Francisco: Ignatius, 1997.

Pinker, Steven. *The Stuff of Thought: Language as a Window into Human Nature*. New York: Penguin, 2007.

Poerksen, Uwe. *Plastic Words: The Tyranny of a Modular Language*. University Park, PA: Pennsylvania State University Press, 1988.

Postman, Neil. *Amusing Ourselves to Death: Public Discourse in the Age of Show Business*. New York: Penguin, 1985.

———. *Technopoly: The Surrender of Culture to Technology*. New York: Vintage, 1993.

Putnam, Robert D. *Bowling Alone: The Collapse and Revival of American Community*. New York: Simon and Schuster, 2000.

Putnam, Robert D., and David E. Campbell. *American Grace: How Religion Divides and Unites Us*. New York: Simon and Schuster, 2010.

Rafaeli, Sheizaf. "Interactivity: From new media to communication." In *Advancing Communication Science: Merging Mass and Interpersonal Process*, edited by Robert P. Hawkins et al., 110–34. Newbury Park, CA: Sage, 1988.

Reitman, Janet. "Inside Scientology: Unlocking the complex code of America's most mysterious religion." *Rolling Stone*, no. 995 (February 8, 2011). http://www.rollingstone.com/culture/news/inside-scientology-20110208.

Roberts, Richard. *Oral Roberts Ministries*. http://oralroberts.com/.

———. "Salvation." *Oral Roberts Ministries*. http://oralroberts.com/teaching/salvation/

Schneider, Fred B., ed. *Trust in Cyberspace*. National Research Council. Washington, DC: National Academies Press, 1999.

Schuller, Robert. *Self Esteem: The New Reformation*. New York: Word, 1982.

Schumacher, E. F. *Small is Beautiful: A Study of Economics as if People Mattered*. New York: Random House, 1973.

Shakespeare, William. *As You Like It*. In *The Riverside Shakespeare: The Complete Works*, 365–402. 2nd ed. Boston: Houghton Mifflin Company, 1997.

———. *Hamlet*. In *The Riverside Shakespeare: The Complete Works*, 1135–1197. 2nd ed. Boston: Houghton Mifflin Company, 1997.

Shirer, William L. *The Rise and Fall of the Third Reich*. New York: Simon and Schuster, 1960.

Soskice, Janet. "Speech bearers: The divine in the human." *The Christian Century*, vol. 133, no. 8 (April 13, 2016). https://www.christiancentury.org/article/2016-03/speech-bearers.

Stivers, Richard. *The Culture of Cynicism: American Morality in Decline*. Cambridge: Blackwell, 1994.

Bibliography

———. *Technology as Magic: The Triumph of the Irrational.* New York: Continuum, 2001.

Susskind, Richard. *The Future of the Law: Facing the Challenges of Information Technology.* Oxford: Oxford University Press, 1996.

———. *Transforming the Law: Essays on Technology, Justice, and the Legal Marketplace.* Oxford: Oxford University Press, 2000.

Sweet, Leonard. *Soul Tsunami: Sink or Swim in the New Millennium Culture.* Grand Rapids: Zondervan, 1999.

Sztompka, Piotr. *Trust: A Sociological Theory.* Cambridge: Cambridge University Press, 1999.

Tappert, Theodore, ed. *The Book of Concord.* Philadelphia: Muhlenberg, 1959.

Tuan, Yi-Fu. *Topophilia: A Study of Environmental Perception, Attitudes, and Values.* Englewood Cliffs, NJ: Prentice-Hall, 1974.

Uslaner, Eric. *Trust as a Moral Value.* Speech, University of Exeter, UK, September 2001. http://www.bsos.umd.edu/gvpt/uslaner/uslanerexeter.pdf.

———. "Trust as a Moral Value." In *The Handbook of Social Capital,* edited by Dario Castiglione et al., 101–21. New York: Oxford University Press, 2008.

Vaillant, George. *Spiritual Evolution: How We Are Wired for Faith, Hope, and Love.* New York: Broadway, 2008.

Vanderburg, Willem. *The Labyrinth of Technology.* Toronto: University of Toronto Press, 2002.

Vanderwolk, M. "Invisible Communities." Unpublished paper. 1991.

Vatican. "Ethics in Communication." Vatican City: Pontifical Council for Social Communication, 2000. http://www.vatican.va/roman_curia/pontifical_councils/pccs/documents/rc_pc_pccs_doc_20000530_ethics-communications_en.html.

Von-Wedel, Christine Christ. *Erasmus of Rotterdam: Advocate of a New Christianity.* Erasmus Studies. Toronto: University of Toronto Press, 2013.

Waddle, Ray. "From the editor: 'this very night your soul.'" *Reflections,* vol. 98, no. 2 (Fall 2011) 76–77.

Weber, Max. *Economy and Society.* Vols. 1 and 2. Edited by Guenther Roth and Claus Wittich. Berkeley, CA: University of California Press, 1978.

Welker, Michael. *What Happens in Holy Communion?* Grand Rapids: Eerdmans, 2000.

Williams, Rowan. *Christ on Trial: How the Gospel Unsettles Our Judgement.* Kindle ed. Grand Rapids: Eerdmans, 2003.

Winner, Langdon. "Complexity, Trust, and Terror." *NETFUTURE: Technology and Human Responsibility.* No. 137 (October 22, 2002). http://www.netfuture.org/2002/Oct2202_137.html.

———. *The Whale and the Reactor.* Chicago: The University of Chicago Press, 1986.

Index

Aelred of Rievaulx, 144, 145
American dream, 113–16, 122, 123
American Sociology Review on loss of friends 129, 130
Amish on technological decisions, 23, 164
appropriate use of technology, 6, 7, 23, 45
    as embodied cognition, 72–75, 159, 163–67
Aquinas, Thomas, xiv
associative communities, 32–34, 147–50
Auden, W.H., 122
Augsburg Confession, 40
Augustine
    on language, 45, 48
    on faith, hope, and love, 67
    on friendship, 144, 145
    on Trinity in creation, 56

Babel, 58, 122, 123
Beck, Gene, 56
beloved community, 106–8, 115, 120, 123–25, 167, 168
    as Eucharist meal, 31, 105, 107
Benedict XVI
    on reductionism, 19, 20
    on faith, hope, and love, 67, 76, 77, 98
    on friendship, 143
Bible as Word of God, 56–60

body
    as Body of Christ and bodily resurrection, 31, 40, 41
    in bodily interaction, 32, 71–76, 147–55
    as blessed uncertainty of words, ix, x, 46–48, 52, 67, 68, 122, 123, 161
    as bodily presence, 31, 33
    in first person experience and skilled activity, 72–75
    in The World Beyond your Head, 72–75
Bok, Sissela, 82
Borgmann, Albert, 24, 33, 34
Brady, Matthew, 152
Bright, Billy, 43, 44
Brothers Karamazov, 138, 139
Brown, Peter, 133, 134
Brunner, Emil, 67
Buber, Martin, 40
bullshit, 55, 56

Campus Crusade for Christ, 44
Carnegie, Andrew, 134
Carr, Nicolas, 52
Cassierer, Ernest, x
catfish, 71
charity
    as a business, 135, 136
    history of, 128–36
    Acts 2, 133

Index

Chomsky, Noam, 47, 48
Christian decision-making, x, xiii, xiv, 67, 68, 77, 98, 100, 121, 124–26, 159, 163–67
church
    in Augsburg Confession, vii, 40
    as Body of Christ, 31, 40, 41
    community, 40, 41, 155–56
    Acts 2, 31, 133
    on the Internet, 31, 33, 160
Clinton, Bill, 3, 110–12, 121, 122, 157
Coffin, Henry Sloane, 99
cognitive science, 47, 74, 75
    on profound thought, 49, 50
    in The Shallows, 52
Collins, Francis, 57, 58
community
    Acts 2, 15, 147–61
    associative communities, 32, 149–55
    The Abundant Community, 147–55, 164
    Christian, 155–61
    common story, 96–97, 118, 150, 152
    electronic lacks connections, 40, 41, 147–61
    electronic reduced to transactions, 4, 43, 119, 125, 142
    face-to-face, 15, 40, 41, 49, 72–75, 130, 131
    global, 15, 35, 54–64, 73, 89, 95, 96, 143, 150, 151, 157, 158, 162, 164
    internet churches, 15, 31–34, 41, 150, 160, 161
    local, 33, 40, 41, 147–55
    Matthew 25, 32–46 136
    personal density, 159
computers, ix, x, 10, 41, 42, 68–71, 112
    data bases, 51
connections, 12–15 146, 147, 155, 156
    community, 15, 40, 41, 147–61

Christianity and connections, 27–41, 45, 56–60, 67, 68, 97–100, 155–62
    context, 12–15, 48
    faith, hope, and love connects past and future, xiv, 67, 68, 76–79, 159
    Mondaugen's Law, 159
    nature, 13, 27–31
    place, 13, 15, 16, 31–34, 147–48, 157–59
    reductionism, 12–15, 19
    removed from context, 12–15, 48, 72–75
    time, 14, 15, 34–40, 149, 150, 159
conversation, 15, 49, 64, 78, 137–40, 147–55, 164
    divine-human, x, xiii, 41, 56–60, 64, 152–56
    face to face, 49 15, 70–75
    interaction and interactivity, 66–67, 71, 152, 156, 163–67
    ongoing, 58, 60, 64, 67–69, 71, 77, 161, 164, 166
    public, 71, 152, 156, 163–67
Copeland Kenneth, 42, 43
covenant, 7, 43, 57–60
Crawford, Matthew, 72–75
creation by word, x, 24, 27, 28, 56–58, 74–77
Cross, Jennifer, 148
culture, ix, x, 149, 150, 155–159
    Christ and Culture, 155, 156, 159
    common story, 96, 97, 150
    common sense as faith, 98, 99
    loss of, 72–75, 153
    public conversation, 71, 152, 156, 163–67
    value agnosticism, 12, 37–40, 45, 95
consumer capitalism, 35, 36, 39, 73
customized religion, 37
Cusa, Nicolas, 48
Cyberspace, 32, 73, 94

David Currillo, 30
democracy, 1–7

Index

Dollar, Creflo, 38
Dostoevsky, 138, 139
Dreyfus, Hubert, 33, 39, 73

economy, 71, 35, 70, 73, 98, 112, 119, 131, 133, 150, 157, 158, 162, 164
   consumer capitalism, 95
   efficiency, 10-12, 14, 18, 71, 87, 89-91, 96, 103, 116, 128, 151-53, 162
Eio, Peter, 4, 5 , 7
electronic devices, ix, x, 40, 41, 65, 66
   computers, ix, x, 10, 41, 42, 51, 68-71, 112
   confidence in machine and systems, 91-95
   electronic media, ix, x, 40, 41, 65, 66
   anonymity, 50, 51, 71
   artificial world, 15-18, 46, 72-75
   images, ix, x, 14, 15, 46-48, 50-52, 152
   interactivity, 68-75
   narrow band communication, x, 15, 40, 41, 51, 72-75, 159
   news becomes entertainment, 56
   proliferation of data, 7, 51, 56, 59, 62
   religious research, 32
   replace personal relationships, 15, 31, 40, 41, 50, 89, 92-103, 121, 129, 135, 147-55, 159
   speed, 50
electronic age, 1, 2, 40, 41, 53-56, 60-66
   making relationships transactions, 41, 72, 73, 119, 148
Eliot, T. S., 76
Ellingson, Stephen, 37
Ellul, Jacques, ix, x, 8, 10-12, 15-17, 20, 24, 46-52, 57, 71, 99, 119, 152, 161
   ambiguity, 48, 68
The Humility of the Word, ix, x, 41-48

The Technological Society, 11
embodiment, 31, 32, 44, 72-75, 147-55, 159
environment of techology, 1, 2, 10-18, 48
Erasmus, 57
Erickson, Erick, 81-83, 97, 98
Eucharist meal, 31, 105, 107
expectation, 30, 39, 96, 103, 108-13, 121, 122
experts, 18, 128, 131, 132

face-to-face, 15, 40, 41, 49, 72-75
Facebook, x, 23, 41, 49-51, 88, 130, 131
Faith, 97, 101, 83-85
   American Grace, 88, 89
   common story, 97
   Father's benevolent care, 83, 97
   enabling face basic human problems, 84
   informs, 67, 77, 95, 100, 114, 116, 147, 161, 166
   light on way, 98-100
   Lumen Fidei, 99-100
   Matthew 6: 25-24, 83
   Matthew 25: 34-46, 99
   promise of, 68, 76, 77, 81, 83, 84, 98, 101, 103, 105, 114, 122, 159, 160, 166
   ongoing conversation, 58, 60, 64, 67-69, 71, 77, 161, 164, 166
   rational choice, 89-91
   remembers, 77-79
   residue of traditional values, 89, 90
   social capital, 85-89
   trust and faith, 81-85
faith, hope, and love
   connect past and future with present, xiv, 67, 68, 76-79, 159
   common story, 98, 99
   context, xiii, xiv
   as counter-cultural, 79, 150-55, 158-67

Index

faith, hope, and love (*continued*)
   decision-making, x, xiii, xiv, 67, 68, 77, 98, 100, 121, 124–26, 159, 163–67
   inform and inspire, 67, 77, 114, 116, 147, 161, 166
   interaction, 49, 64–67, 76–79, 96, 101, 121–23, 160, 166
   interchangeable, 67–75
   Lumen Fidei, 98–100
   meaning and purpose, 18, 19, 67, 98, 139
   narrative of salvation, 63
   overcome cynicism, fatalism, fear, 80
   story and promise, memory and promise, 76
   trichromonizing, 74, 75
Falwell, Jerry, 114
familiarity, 89–93
Ferber, Paul, 68–72
financial crisis, 2008 16, 94, 95
Foltz, Franz, ix, 22, 30, 68–72, 32, 33, 119, 135, 149, 150
Foltz and Foltz, ix, xiv, 30, 32, 33, 119, 135, 149, 150
Ferber, Foltz, and Pugliese
   on interaction, 68–72
   consumer capitalism, 73
for the time being, 122
forgiveness, 30, 137, 141, 142, 167
fragility of technology, 93–96
Francis I Lumen Fidei, 98–100
Frankfurt, Henry, 55, 56
friendship, 143–45
   face-to-face, 15, 40, 41, 49, 72–75, 130, 131
   professional, 131
Froese, Paul, 114
Fukuyama, Francis, 87
Fullilove, Mindy Thompson, 148
futurists, 108, 109
   Steve Kurzweil, 108, 109, 121, 122
   Age of Spiritual Machine, 108, 109
   singularity, 109, 157

computers smarter than humans, 108, 109

Giddens, Anthony
   on friendship, 145
   protective cocoons, 95, 96
   intimacy, 129, 130
   new common story, 96, 98, 99
globalism, 15, 35, 54–64, 73, 89, 95, 96, 143, 150, 151, 157, 158, 162, 164
God
   in Large Catechism as great speaker, 56
   Word of God, 56–60
grace
   infused, xiii
   Romans 5:11, 137, 138
Greenspan, Alan, 94, 95

Ha, Louisa, 69
Haekel, Stephan H., 69
Hall, John Douglas, 79
Hammon, David, 148
Hardin, Russell, 90, 91
Hart, David Bentley, 137, 138
Hauerwaus, Stanley
   grain of universe, 27
   friendship, 145
Heeter, Carrie, 69
Hefner, Philip, 13
highway system, 8, 9
hope, 114, 116, 121
   Age of Spiritual Machine, 108, 109
   beloved community, 106–8
   expectation, 30, 39, 96, 103, 108–13, 121, 122
   For the Time Being, 122
   I Have A Dream, 114–17, 122, 123
   inspires, 67, 77, 114, 116, 121–23, 147, 161, 166
   Just Society, 105, 106, 122, 123
   optimism, 39, 96, 102, 103, 110–12, 119, 120

Index

Pandora's Box, 102, 103, 122, 123, 133, 134, 153, 155
Peaceable Kingdom, 104
North Haven, 21, 22, 45
visions of the future, 103–8
visions of technology, 108–12
Humiliation of the Word, ix, 46–48, 52
  bullshit, 55, 56
  commonplaces, 54
  newspeak, 53
  propaganda, 54
  plastic words, 53–55
  replaced by images, ix, x, 14, 15, 46–48, 50–52, 152
  uniquack, 55

I-Thou Buber, 40
Illich, Ivan, xiv, 15–17, 20, 133
  Corruption of the best, 25, 26
  critique of technology, 10–12
  death of words, 52
  friendship, 145
  institutionalization, 9, 11, 15–17
  inverse of Christianity, 25, 26
  Moloch system, 25, 26
  Pandora's Box, 102, 103, 122, 123, 133, 134, 154, 155
  reading aloud, 49
  uniquack, 55
images replace words, ix, x, 14, 15, 46–48, 50–52, 152
  graven images, 59
immediacy, 50–52, 159
incarnation, 32
  embodiment, 31–33, 44, 72–75, 147–55, 159
interaction and interactivity, 68–71, 76
  face-to-face, 15, 39–41, 49, 49, 72–75
  of faith, hope, and love, 49, 64–67, 76–79, 96, 101, 121–23, 160, 166
  in machine moderated communication, 40, 41, 65, 66, 71–76

Internet community, 32, 33, 40, 41, 150–55
Internet churches, 15, 32–34, 41, 160, 161
intimacy, 129, 130

James, E. Lincoln, 69
Jefferson, Thomas, 3, 6
Jenson, Robert, 19
  faith, hope, and love rhyming past and future with present, 76, 77
  God as speaker, 56, 57
  on online community, 33, 41
  on the story of Western Civilization, 64
Just Society, 105, 106
justice, 117–20
  distributive, 119
  The Future of Law, 119, 120
  Juridification, 119
  Torah, 118

Kennedy, John F, 2–4, 6, 7, 12, 163
King, Martin Luther, 120, 122, 123–25, 127, 137, 140, 142, 114–16, 156, 160
  Beloved Community, 114–16, 120
  critique, 114–16
  Christianity and the American Dream, 113–16, 122, 123
  love your enemy, 124, 125
  We Shall Overcome, 113–16, 117
Kiousis, Spiro, 69
Kropp, Paul, 52
Kurzweil, Ray, 108, 109, 121, 122, 157

LaHay, Tim, 105
Lamesh no revenge, 141
language ambiguity, ix, 46–48
  Babel, x, 58, 122, 123
  blessed uncertainty, ix, x, 46–48, 52, 67, 68, 122, 123, 161
  common sense, 47
  create meaning, 45, 47
  crisis in, ix, x, 46–48, 51, 52

INDEX

language ambiguity (*continued*)
   electronic, 50–52, 62–64
   history of, 49–52
   naming, 47
   narrative, 47, 48
   oral, x, 49, 61, 62
   order to chaos, 47, 56, 57
   replaced by images, ix, x, 14, 15, 46–48, 50–52, 152
   written, 49, 50, 61, 62, 81
Large Catechism
   on trust, 84
   God as speaker, 56, 57
law of prosperity, 30, 42
laws of creation, 30, 31, 39, 42, 43, 53, 97
liberation theology, 36
Limbaugh, Rush, 56
Lindbeck, George, 19
Lindberg, Carter, 133, 134
local community, 33, 40, 41, 147–50, 157, 158
logos, 25, 56, 57, 155, 156
love, 124–28, 137–42
   abundance, 124, 125
   agape, 137–42
   caring, 124, 160
   charity, 133–35
   Christian, 124–28, 137–42
   comprehensive
   I John 4: 7–12, 127, 128
   I Corinthians 13, 125
   compassion suffer, 124, 125, 137, 139
   covenant, 137, 138
   forgiveness, 30, 137, 141, 142, 16
   friendship, 143–45
   God in I John 4:8, 127
   great command, 126
   intimacy, 128–32
   love your enemies, 124, 125, 137, 138
   make enemies friends, 124, 125
   New Testament, 125–28
   no revenge, 141
   nonviolent, 137, 141
   pure relationships, 129–31
   redemptive change agent, 124–28, 137–43
   return good for evil, 124, 125
   sacrifice, 137–39
   Shema, 126
   in technology, 128–32
   transformative, 124, 125, 137–39
   unconditional love, 137, 138
Low Setha, 148
Luhmann, Niklas
   confidence in system not people, 91–93, 95
   familiarity trust confidence, 91–93
   friendship, 145
   intimacy, 129, 130
Lukes, Steven, 153–55
Lumen Fidei, 98–100
Luther, Martin, xiv
   on faith, 67, 84
   God as speaker, 56, 57
   priority of the spoken word, 61, 62
   theology of cross, xiv

machine moderated communication, x, 40, 41, 65, 66, 71–76
Mansbridge, Jane, 82, 87, 88
Maximos the Confessor, 139
McGovern, G., 70
McKibben, Bill, 13
McKnight, John and Block, Peter, 164
McLuhan, Marshall, 71
McNamara, Robert, 3
meaning and purpose, 62, 64, 67, 139, 149, 165
   eliminated in technology, x, 16
   in words, 46–48, 64, 65
milieu technique, 1, 2, 10–16, 37, 39, 42, 72–74, 79, 109, 128, 147
   challenge from faith, hope, and love, 150–55, 158–67
   replace words with images, ix, x, 14, 15, 46–48, 50–52, 152
Moloch society, 25, 26
Mondaugen's Law on personal density, 159

INDEX

Moral Majority, 136
Moses, Robert, 17
Murphy, Nancy, 31

narrative, 47, 48, 68
   realistic, 56, 63, 157, 158
nature, 13, 27–31
   The End of Nature, 13
   God revealed in, 27, 28
   benevolent/ indifferent, 27, 28
   laws of creation not nature, 30, 31, 42, 43, 53, 96, 97, 113
natural law, 29, 42, 43
newspeak, 53
Nicolas of Cusa, 48
Niebuhr, H. Richard
   Christ and Culture, 155, 156
   Faith, 85
Noble, David, 24
Nordvall, Robert, 37
North Haven millennium celebration, 21, 22, 45
NRA, 16, 95, 154

Ooze, 32
Obama, Barach, 5–7 165
optimism, 39, 96, 102, 103, 110–12, 119, 120
oral stage, 49, 60, 61
Orwell, George, 53
Osteen, Joel, 39, 96, 113

Pandora's Box, 102, 103, 122, 123, 133, 134, 153, 155
Peaceable Kingdom, 104
Peale, Norman Vincent, 39, 96, 113
Pentecostal, 38, 60
Pew Religious Landscape study
   church attendance, 86
Pieper, Joseph, 67
Pinker, Stephen, 47, 74, 75
place, 13, 15, 16, 31–34, 147–48, 157–59
plan for salvation, 37, 43, 44, 96, 113,
plastic words, 53–56
Poerksen, Uwe, 54, 55

Postman, Neil, 17, 18, 56
power of positive thinking, 39, 96, 113
power over against love, 142
professional friend, 55, 131, 133
principalities and powers, 24, 25 156
   Col 1: 15–20, I Corinthians 15:26–28, 24, 25
proliferation of data, 7, 51, 56, 59, 62
promise of faith, 68, 76, 77, 81, 83, 84, 98, 101, 103, 105, 114, 122, 159, 160, 166 promise of technology, 7, 21, 32, 89, 96
propaganda, 54
public conversation, 71, 152, 156, 163–67
Pugliese, Rudy, 68–72
Putnam, Robert, 88, 89, 146
   American Grace: How Religion Unites and Divides Us, 88, 89
   Bowling Alone, 46

radical individualism, 160
Rafaeli, Sheizaf, 68
rational choice school, 89–91
reality, 46
reductionism, 10–16, 19, 20, 155–57
relationships conversation, 56–60, 64
   connections, 10–16, 27–41, 40, 41, 147–50, 155–61
   human, 158, 159
   human-divine, x, xiii, xiv, 41–43, 56–60, 64, 152–56
rhyme past and future, 76, 77
risk management, 89–91
Roberts, Oral, 38
Roberts, Richard, 42
Robinson Pat, 113
Rothblatt, Martine, 109
Roy, Rustum, xi, xiv, 24

sabbath lifestyle, 34, 35
salvation, ix, 24, 25, 30, 34, 42–44, 59, 60, 63, 96, 117, 123, 159, 161, 166
sacrifice, 137, 139–41
scarcity of love, 121, 124, 125, 129–30

Index

Schuller, Robert, 39, 96, 113
Schumaker E F, 164
Scientology, 38, 39
Security
    Defense Advanced Research
        Projects Agency, 93
    Drop Your Arms, 151
    just war theory, 16
    mutually assured destruction,
        153, 155
    National Security Agency, 93
    Weapons, 16, 93–85, 122
Seed, law of, 40
self- denial, 124, 125, 127, 137–39
Shakespeare, William, 13, 50, 56
Shirer, William, 17
singularity
    Kurzweil on the future, 109, 157
    Uniqueness, 19, 48, 79, 156
social capital, 85–89
social media, x, 41, 50–52, 65, 66,
    130, 131,
solidarity, 35, 133, 134, 143, 145
Soskice, Janet, 58
Specialists, 18, 128, 131, 132
Speer, Albert, 17
spirituality as health, 29, 39
Stivers, Richard, xi, 11, 12, 122
story and promise, 46–48 68, 76, 77,
    98, 99, 114–17
suffering, 124, 125, 137–39
Susskind, David, 119, 120
Sweet, Leonard, 22
systems, 15, 16
    insecurity and vulnerability of
        systems, 93–96
    too big to fail, 15, 16

Taittiriya Brahm, x
Technique, 10–18 46–48, 51, 52, 64,
    72–75, 128–35, 137, 153–67
    destroys meaning of religious
        words, 45
    faith, hope, and love challenge,
        79, 150–55, 158–67
    milieu technique shapes the
        meaning of words, 45, 53–56

reductionism, 10–16, 128, 155–57
religious practice and teaching,
    36–39
    on succumbing to technique, 37,
        39, 42, 96
techniques, 11
technocracy, 18
technological environment, 1, 2,
    10–12, 15, 41–46
    artificial world, 13, 14
    fundamentalism scientism, 57, 63
    highway system, 8, 9
technology
    all pervasive, 2, 10–12
    appropriate use of, 45, 163–67
    artificial world, 13, 14, 46, 72–75
    business model, 35, 36, 42, 43,
        131, 132, 135, 136
    consumer capitalism, 73
    degrade tradition, ix, 11, 34–39,
        45
    distraction, 5,72, 73, 75
    divides churches, 21, 22
    efficiency, 10–12, 14, 18, 71, 96,
        103, 128, 151–53, 162
    experts, 18, 128, 131, 132
    immediacy, 22, 159
    images, x, 46–48
    liberates, 28
    no future, 22, 159
    solves all problems, 2–7, 11, 12,
        121, 162
    specialization, 18, 128, 131, 132
    as tool, 2
    value agnosticism, 12, 37–40, 45,
        72–74, 95
    and words, ix, 46–48, 53–56
technology and magic, 12
    environment, 1, 2, 11, 14
    solves all, 6, 7 27, 28, 72–4
technology in the Church, 14–16, 22,
    23, 41–45
televangelists, 32, 33, 41–45
terrorism vulnerable technology, 25
textual, 49, 50, 61
theology nature of doctrine, 19
    customized, 37

Index

practice above doctrine, 36–39
Tillich, Paul, 19
Time, 13, 14, 34–40, 149, 150, 159
tools, 2
tradition
    church, 37–40, 45
    familiarity, 71, 89–92, 96, 97, 163
    technology degrades, 6, 7, 37–40, 45
    trust, 80–85
trust
    altruistic, 87, 88
    basic to everyday life, 80–85
    confidence in technological system, 91–93
    crisis, 91–93
    eBay, 90, 91
    encapsulated interest, 90, 91
    faith, 80–85
    familiarity, trust, confidence, 91–93
    rational choice, 89–91
    social virtues and prosperity, 87
    World Values Survey, 85
    social capital, 85–89
truth search for, 182
Tuan, Yi-Fu, 148

uniquack, 55
Uslaner, Eric, 88, 89

Vaillant, George, 74, 75
value agnosticism, 12, 37–40, 45, 72–74, 95
Vandenberg, William, 12
Vatican
    on online communication, 34
    on liberation theology, 36
virtual reality, 41, 42, 152
    as the Enlightenment project, 72–75
virtues cardinal, xiii, xiv, 3, 163, 166
visions of the future, 103–7
    technology, 108–12
    Martin Luther King, x, 114–17

wellness, 28, 29
Williams, Rowan, 77, 78
Winner, Langdon, 17
    The Whale and Reactor, 46, 47, 151
vulnerable systems, 93, 94
Wittgenstein, Ludwig, 99
words
    ambiguity, ix, x, 45, 47, 48, 68
    blessed uncertainty, ix, x, 46–48, 52, 67, 68, 122, 123, 161
    common sense, 47, 48
    create meaning, 45–48, 64, 65
    in creation, x, 56–60
    crisis, ix, x, 52, 53
    death of, 52
    God, 56–60
    identify who we are, xiv, 48
    logos, 56, 57
    naming, 47
    oral stage, 49
    plastic, 53–56
    as salvation, ix, x, 56–60
    search for truth, 46, 48
    spoken, x, 49, 61, 62
    Word of God, 56–60
words of knowledge, 63
    technology destroys meaning, 45, 51, 52, 53–56
    technology removes from connections, 45, 47, 48, 53–56, 155–61
World Values Survey, 85
written text, 49, 50, 61, 81

Zosima, 135, 139